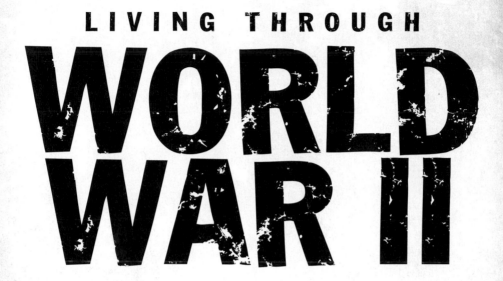

LIVING THROUGH
WORLD WAR II

Andrew Langley

Heinemann
LIBRARY
Chicago, Illinois

www.capstonepub.com
Visit our website to find out
more information about
Heinemann-Raintree books.

To order:

☎ Phone 888-454-2279

🖳 Visit www.capstonepub.com
to browse our catalog and order online.

Edited by Andrew Farrow, Adam Miller,
 and Vaarunika Dharmapala
Designed by Steve Mead
Original illustrations © Capstone Global
 Ltd 2012
Illustrations by Jeff Edwards
Picture research by Ruth Blair
Originated by Capstone Global Library Ltd
Printed and bound in the USA

15 14 13 12 11
10 9 8 7 6 5 4 3 2 1

**Library of Congress Cataloging-in-
Publication Data**
Langley, Andrew.
 World War II / Andrew Langley.
   p. cm.—(Living through—)
 Includes bibliographical references and
index.
  ISBN 978-1-4329-6002-5 (hb)—ISBN 978-
1-4329-6011-7 (pb) 1. World War, 1939-
1945—Juvenile literature. I. Title. II. Title:
World War Two. III. Title: World War 2.
  D743.7.L36 2012
  940.53—dc23   2011016056

Acknowledgments
We would like to thank the following
for permission to reproduce photographs:
akg-images pp. 13, 55 (IAM), 31, 59 (ullstein
bild), 10, 25, 37, 47, 61, 63; © Australian War
Memorial p. 32; © Corbis pp. 19, 35; Corbis
pp. 5 (© Bettmann), 41 (© Hulton-Deutsch
Collection); Getty Images pp. 9, 48 (Galerie
Bilderwelt), 15, 65 (FPG/Hulton Archive),
21, 39 (Popperfoto), 26 (SSPL), 42 (Apic),
50 (Roger Viollet), 53 (AFP); Mary Evans
pp. 7, 23.

Cover photograph reproduced with the
permission of Getty Images (Kenneth
Rittener/Rittener).

Michael Bruce quoted in Leonard Baker, *Days
of Sorrow and Pain* (OUP, 1978) 80 words
from p. 231. © Leonard Baker. Reprinted by
permission of Oxford University Press, Inc.

CONTENTS

Words printed in **bold** are explained in the glossary.

THE PATH TO WAR

The battles of World War II took place from Europe to North Africa and the Pacific Islands. Soldiers fought in jungles, deserts, woods, and snowfields, as well as in the air and at sea. At least 50 million people died in the war,[1] and more than half of these were civilians. The fighting also affected the lives of countless millions more.

Around 60 countries took part in World War II. (The remainder stayed **neutral**.) On one side were the Axis powers. These were led by Germany, Japan, and Italy. Six other nations joined the Axis during the war, including Hungary, Bulgaria, and Romania. On the other side were the Allies. The major Allied powers were the United States, the United Kingdom, China, and the **Soviet Union**. Among the other Allies were France, Australia, Canada, India, Greece, and Yugoslavia.

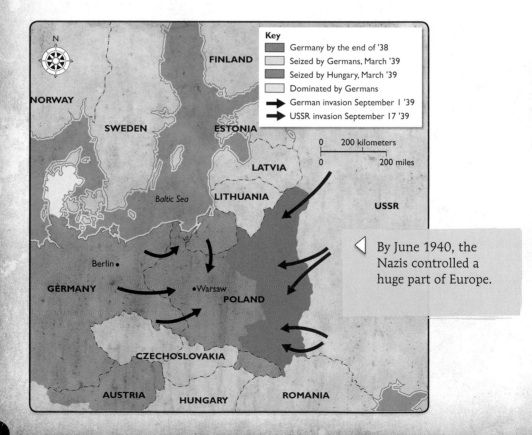

By June 1940, the Nazis controlled a huge part of Europe.

CAUSES OF THE WAR

World War I (1914–18) ended with German defeat and the signing of the Treaty of Versailles in 1919. This took away Germany's overseas colonies and territory in Europe, and it forced Germany to pay compensation for war damage. The original sum was $63 billion, and Germany had to take out a loan to pay this, while being charged interest. Germany was finally able to repay this in October 2010.[2]

World War I crippled most European economies. This, combined with other problems, led to an economic **depression** throughout the world. The Great Depression, as it became known, caused mass unemployment, poverty, and social unrest in many countries during the 1930s.

THE AGE OF DICTATORS

The troubled times allowed the rise of **dictators** in several countries. These were leaders who held total power and crushed all opposition. By the early 1930s, there were dictators ruling many parts of the world, such as Spain, Italy, the Soviet Union, and Japan.

The Germans, bitter over the Versailles Treaty, longed for a strong ruler who would wipe out the shame of defeat. In 1933 Adolf Hitler was appointed their chancellor (prime minister). He was leader of the National Socialists (the **Nazis**), the most powerful political party in the country. Hitler quickly turned Germany into a dictatorship.

BIOGRAPHY

Adolf Hitler, 1889–1945

BORN: Austria

ROLE: Chancellor of Germany and leader of the Nazi Party

Hitler joined the German army in 1914, and he won the Iron Cross for his courage during World War I. He blamed the Jews for Germany's defeat and became a fierce anti-Semite, meaning he was very prejudiced against Jews. In 1920 he helped form the National Socialist (Nazi) Party. The group did not win a majority of votes in the 1933 election, but Hitler was appointed chancellor of Germany.

DID YOU KNOW? As a young man, Hitler wanted to be a painter. A collection of his paintings fetched almost $15,000 at an auction in April 2009.[3]

BREAKING THE TREATY

Hitler transformed Germany. He had two major goals: to create a powerful new German empire, and to rid the country of Jews. During his first three years in power, Hitler changed Germany from a poor, defeated, ashamed nation into a thriving and proud country. Above all, Germany had a powerful new army. Under the Versailles Treaty, the German army was limited to 100,000 men,[4] but Hitler scorned the treaty. By 1936 his army totaled around 400,000.

Hitler broke another condition of the Versailles Treaty that year when his forces marched into a region of Germany called the Rhineland. This area was supposed to be forbidden to the German military. Hitler's first ambition was to regain the territories that Germany had lost during World War I. At this stage, there was little opposition. Britain, France, and other West European powers were anxious to avoid another outbreak of war.

THE FASCIST ALLIANCE

In 1936 Germany also gained its first ally—Italy. Led by Benito Mussolini, Italy had become a **fascist**, **totalitarian** state. Its aims were very similar to Germany's, although without the anti-Jewish policies. Both Hitler and Mussolini were determined to expand their empires, and the Italian army had already invaded Ethiopia, in East Africa.

Hitler's next move was to seize control of neighboring Austria (see the map on page 4). German troops marched into Austria in March 1938 and took control without firing a shot. Many Austrian people welcomed the arrival of the Nazis, because they wanted to be united with Germany. The people spoke the same language, and the two countries had been allies in World War I. Hitler was born in Austria.

The next German target was western Czechoslovakia (see the map on page 4), part of an area called the Sudetenland, where many Germans lived. In desperation, the Czechs appealed for help from the United Kingdom and France. Then in September 1938, Hitler held a meeting in Munich with British and French leaders. Eager to avoid war, they agreed that Hitler should be allowed to take the Sudetenland.

British Prime Minister Neville Chamberlain returned home in triumph, announcing that there would now be "peace in our time."

His policy was known as "appeasement"—keeping the peace by giving concessions to potential enemies. However, Hitler had big plans. In March 1939, his troops invaded not just the Sudetenland, but also all of Czechoslovakia. The United Kingdom and France did nothing in response.

THE RISE OF JAPAN

Meanwhile, on the other side of the world, Japan had begun to expand its empire in Southeast Asia. It had seized the Chinese province of Manchuria in 1931, and in 1937 Japanese forces started a full-scale invasion of China's mainland. They destroyed the major city of Nanking, slaughtering at least 50,000 people.[5]

After a year of brutal fighting, Japan controlled most of eastern China. The Chinese continued to resist the invaders, though. The conflict turned into a long and savage struggle, which cost both sides many lives. It also became part of World War II, lasting until 1945 and tying up large numbers of Japanese troops.

▽ Adolf Hitler returns the salutes of a crowd of followers at Nuremberg, Germany, in 1936.

FIRST MOVES AGAINST JEWS

One of the main aims of the Nazi Party was to rid Germany of its Jewish population.

As soon as Hitler came to power in 1933, he began a program of persecution against Jews, gypsies, homosexuals, and other minorities. This soon developed into a campaign of **genocide**, leading to the horrors of the death camps and the **Holocaust**.

WHY DID HITLER PERSECUTE JEWISH PEOPLE?

Hitler expressed his hatred for the Jews as early as 1920. In a speech, he said, "The poisoning of the people will not end as long as the Jew is not removed from our midst."[6] He blamed Jews for causing Germany to lose World War I, and he accused them of conspiring with the communists in Russia to take over the world.

Hitler and other Nazis believed that true Germans ("Aryans") were a superior race, and Jews were inferior. They felt that Jews not only threatened the health of German society, but also occupied land needed by others.

THE NUREMBERG LAWS AND AFTER

Beginning in 1935, Hitler passed a series of laws that deprived Jews of many rights, seized their property, and isolated them from the rest of society. Some of the major results of these laws were:
• Marriages between Jews and Germans were forbidden.
• Jews were not classified as German citizens.
• Jewish employees were dismissed from their jobs.
• Aryans took over companies run and owned by Jews.

On November 9, 1938, Nazi storm troopers attacked Jewish factories, stores, and homes all over Germany and Austria. At least 100 German Jews were killed[7] and many buildings were destroyed. The streets were so littered with shattered glass that the atrocity became known as *Kristallnacht* ("crystal night").

◁ During the time of *Kristallnacht*, Jewish women in Linz, Austria, were forced to hold up signs reading, "I have been excluded from the national community."

Journalist Michael Bruce described one violent incident of that night:

The streets were a chaos of screaming bloodthirsty people. The object of the mob's hate was a hospital for sick Jewish children, many of them cripples or consumptives [suffering from serious lung disease]. In minutes the windows had been smashed and the doors forced. When we arrived, the swine were driving the wee mites out over the broken glass, bare-footed and wearing nothing but their nightshirts. The nurses, doctors, and attendants were being kicked and beaten by the mob leaders, most of whom were women.[8]

Geniuses in exile

The persecution of the Jews caused a "talent drain" in German society. Thousands of Jews, and other persecuted people, fled the country and went to live abroad. Among them were many brilliant and gifted people. These included the physicist Albert Einstein, psychiatrist Sigmund Freud, and composer Kurt Weill. Germany also lost leading scientists who would help develop the atomic bomb in the United States, such as Leo Szilard, Lise Meitner, and Edward Teller.

A LIGHTNING WAR

By the spring of 1939, it seemed that a war in Europe was inevitable. The British and French governments realized that Hitler had very ambitious plans for Germany and was building up his armed forces rapidly. He was clearly prepared to ignore treaties and deceive other countries in order to get his way. The Germans were also rearming much more quickly than the United Kingdom and France.

TAKING SIDES

After the easy triumph in Czechoslovakia, the Germans turned their attention to Poland and threatened to seize the port of Gdansk. At last, the British and French actively opposed Hitler's plans. They announced that they would come to Poland's aid if Germany attacked it.

Hitler was furious, and he continued to prepare for an invasion of Poland. However, he had one major problem— would the Soviet Union also fight in support of the Poles? By August 1939 Hitler had persuaded the Soviet leader, Joseph Stalin, to sign a pact (treaty) declaring that the two countries would not go to war against each other. In secret, Hitler and Stalin agreed to split Poland between them.

△ German motorcycle units were an essential part of the invasion of Poland in 1939, speeding soldiers deep into enemy territory.

WAR IS DECLARED

Early on the morning of September 1, 1939, the first German tanks crossed the border into Poland (see the map on page 4). They had soon driven deep into the Polish defenses. At the same time, bombers destroyed the airfields and their planes, crippling the Polish air force.

On September 3, the British and French governments declared war on Germany. Immediately, they began making final preparations. Reserve soldiers were called up to the army. The production of aircraft and other weapons was increased. Children from London and other big cities were **evacuated** to areas that would be safe from bombing.

The German army and air force smashed its way across Poland, burning villages and slaughtering thousands of civilians. Following behind them was a special force called the SS (*Schutzstaffel*, or "Protective Squadron"). Its job was to stamp out all opposition to Nazi rule, and to round up Jews and other minorities.

Soon Poland was being invaded from both sides. On September 17, Soviet troops attacked from the east. By the end of the month, the entire country was divided between the Germans and the Soviets. By Christmas, the Soviet "Red Army" had also invaded Finland.

THE PHONY WAR

At this point, Hitler's plan was simple. He wanted to complete the German conquests in western Europe as quickly as possible. Then he could begin his main task—to expand German territories into the east and create more *lebensraum* (German for "living room") for the Aryan empire. However, after the triumph in Poland, the German army needed time to recover and build up its strength again.

Meanwhile, the Allies could do little except watch the Polish agony. Their forces were still weak, so they were recruiting new soldiers, sailors, and pilots, as well as building up their weapons, as quickly as possible. The French army had moved troops to defend the Maginot Line—a fortified stretch of the border with Germany. A small force of British troops had arrived in northern France. Throughout the early months of 1940, there was very little fighting in western Europe. This period became known as the Phony War.

TIGHTENING THE GRIP

However, other threats were growing. In February 1940, Hitler ordered a blockade of the seas around the United Kingdom. His U-boats (submarines) attacked cargo ships sailing there, with the aim of preventing food and other supplies from reaching the country. In the same month, Finland surrendered to the Soviets.

German land forces rolled forward again in April, when they invaded Denmark and then Norway (see the map on page 16). This took the British by surprise. The British sent battleships and troops to help the Norwegians, but it was too late. Within a few weeks, Germany had taken full control and secured important bases for its U-boats and aircraft.

CHURCHILL TAKES OVER

The Allies were forced to retreat from Norway. The failure of the operation caused outrage in the United Kingdom. Worse still, it was clear that the Germans were getting ready to attack France. Prime minister Neville Chamberlain resigned, and on May 10, he was replaced by Winston Churchill. Churchill immediately appointed a new cabinet (team of advisers) consisting of politicians from all the major parties.

BIOGRAPHY

Winston Churchill,
1874–1965

BORN: England

ROLE: Prime minister of the United Kingdom (1940–45 and 1951–55)

Churchill had already had a long political career when he became prime minister of the United Kingdom. He first entered **Parliament** in 1900. He became First Lord of the Admiralty (in charge of the Royal Navy) in 1911, and during World War I he served in the war cabinet (council). In the 1920s, he campaigned for the overthrow of the Soviet government in Russia. During the 1930s, he was a leading opponent of the government's policy of "appeasement" (trying to make peace with Germany in order to avoid another war).

DID YOU KNOW? Churchill served as a member of Parliament in the United Kingdom for more than 60 years—19 of them after World War II. He finally retired in 1964.

On the same day, Hitler launched his forces into what were known as the Low Countries: Holland (the Netherlands), Belgium, and Luxembourg (see the map on page 16). Headed once again by fast tanks and armored troop-carriers, the advance smashed through enemy defenses. Within a week, both Luxembourg and the Netherlands had surrendered. On May 28, the Belgians also surrendered. Suddenly, events had begun to happen very quickly.

British and French troops hurried north in France to meet the threat, but again they were outwitted. The German invaders took them by surprise, breaking through the thinly defended area of the Ardennes forest and then circling around behind the advancing Allies. By late May, the Allies were almost surrounded and had been driven back to the French coast. Many assembled at the port of Dunkirk, near the Belgian border. From here, more than 337,000[1] were ferried to England on naval ships, helped also by fishing boats, yachts, and other private vessels. The rescue of the troops was a near miracle, but all of their equipment was left behind.

◁ Following the invasion of France in 1940, many thousands of British and French troops were rescued from Dunkirk and ferried to safety in England.

FACING THE BLITZKRIEG

The beginning of World War II brought a brand new word—*blitzkrieg*, the German word for "lightning war." This was a method of fast and ferocious attack, using tanks and other modern armaments. The speed of the assault shocked and bewildered the enemy, who could not react swiftly enough. It also brought quick results—the German army defeated the Low Countries and France in just seven weeks.

TANKS AND TERROR

The success of *blitzkrieg* was not due to greater numbers or better weapons. It came from speed and precise organization, using the modern technology of the time.

- Light, modern tanks could move faster than British or French machines. The Germans grouped them in armored units, which could operate independently. This made them more flexible and effective than Allied tanks, which were only used to support ground troops.
- Troop carriers, trucks, and even motorcycles carried infantry units.
- Special forces landed by parachute to secure crucial sites.
- "Stuka" dive bombers, which used loud sirens as they attacked, caused panic among enemy soldiers and **refugees**.
- Radio allowed commanders to communicate and make instant decisions.
- Engineers built bridges over rivers and blew up obstacles.

Did you know?

The Nazis did not invent the idea of *blitzkrieg*. They had actually copied the method from the Allies in World War I. On August 8, 1918, British, U.S., and other Allied forces broke through the German lines near Amiens, France, with tanks. The Germans learned from the success of this advance, and from the new developments in tank warfare during the 1920s and 1930s. The Allies did not adapt as quickly to these new techniques.

▽ Carrying as many possessions as possible, French civilians fled south on foot from the advancing Germans.

FLEEING THE FIGHTING

Blitzkrieg was terrifying for enemy soldiers, facing racing tanks on the ground and dive bombers screaming overhead. It must have been much worse though for civilians, who might suddenly find themselves on the front line of a battle. Their homes and their lives were in great danger, even though they were not taking part in the fighting.

The only escape for people in attacked areas at this time was to leave their houses and hurry south, away from the advancing Germans. The lucky ones had cars or bicycles. Others loaded their belongings onto wheelbarrows or their backs. These refugees filled the roads in endless lines, sometimes blocking the way of troops.

Terror and panic were never far away. Some refugees were bombed and machine-gunned by Nazi aircraft. Others became separated from their families. Tired, hungry, and lost, they spread confusion across the country. A British soldier described refugees in northern France:

Many women were in the last stages of exhaustion, many of them with their feet tied up with string and brown paper where their shoes had given out. Like one big wave, the whole of this humanity, short of food and sleep and terrified to the core, was congesting [blocking] all roads.[2]

THE FALL OF FRANCE

After Dunkirk, there was little to stop the German advance into the heart of France. In early June 1940, Nazi forces smashed through the French and British armies. By June 14, the Nazis controlled the French capital, Paris. A **swastika** flag was raised over the Eiffel Tower. Many Parisians fled south, leaving the streets empty and silent.

The month of June brought nothing but bad news for the Allies. The conflict in northern Europe was a glorious triumph for the Germans. Now Italy joined them, declaring war on the United Kingdom and France. Soviet troops invaded Lithuania and the other Baltic states (see the map below). In East Asia, the Japanese continued their advance deep into southern China—although in Europe, little notice was taken of this at the time.

France surrendered on June 18. Four days later, French leaders agreed to an **armistice**. Hitler arranged for them to sign the armistice documents in a railroad car at Compiegne, near Paris. In 1918 the Germans had been forced to sign their surrender in the same car.

The war was only 10 months old, yet already the Axis powers (Germany and Italy) controlled most of Europe. The Soviet Union

▷ This map shows Europe in July 1940.

Axis nations

Nations and areas controlled by Axis Powers

Allied nations occupied by Axis Powers

Nations and areas controlled by Soviet Union

Allied nations occupied by Soviet Union

Allied nations and nations and areas under Allied control

Neutral nations

Vichy France and nations under Vichy control

was tightening its grip in the east. There were fears that Spain, led by its fascist dictator, General Franco, might join Germany's side. This left the United Kingdom almost alone in Europe, but supported by distant nations of its empire like Canada and Australia.

Hitler was sure Churchill would make peace with Germany now that France had fallen. However, the British continued fighting. Churchill had told Parliament, "We shall go on to the end.... We shall never surrender." In July, British ships attacked the French fleet at Oran in North Africa, to keep it out of German hands.

Free French

Not all the French soldiers had given up. General Charles de Gaulle had escaped to London, and he rallied others to continue the fight against Germany as the "Free French." Soon, the Free French forces included other refugees and troops from France's colonies in Africa. They took part in many campaigns throughout the war, including the D-Day landings in Normandy in 1944 (see pages 50–53).

The United Kingdom began to prepare for a German invasion. The shores of the south and east coasts were lined with barbed wire and gun **bunkers**. Concrete "pillboxes" (block houses) and obstacles were built at strategic points. For example, some open spaces were filled with old cars to prevent enemy gliders from landing.

U.S. NEUTRALITY

After the horrific experience of World War I, many Americans did not want their soldiers to die in another European conflict. They saw this as a struggle between old-fashioned imperial powers that need not involve them. There were also many German-Americans who supported the aims of the Axis powers, as well as a significant minority who sympathized with Hitler's anti-Jewish aims.

However, the German conquests in western Europe and the threat to the United Kingdom made U.S. leaders nervous. President Franklin D. Roosevelt warned that dictators, such as Hitler and Mussolini, had to be resisted if liberty was to be preserved. A Europe dominated by the Nazis would be a threat to the United States. In mid-July, Roosevelt began to build U.S. naval strength in the Pacific and the Atlantic. He also agreed to sell U.S. weapons and aircraft to the United Kingdom.

STRUGGLE TO SURVIVE

In July 1940, Hitler ordered his commanders to plan the invasion of the United Kingdom, to be called Operation Sealion. He insisted that the first step was to destroy the British Royal Air Force. This would leave the way clear for German troops to cross the English Channel by sea and by air (with special forces landing by parachute). Privately, Hitler believed that defeat in the air would persuade the British to make peace without the need for an invasion at all.[1]

The first German bomber appeared over the United Kingdom on July 6. Its target was an army camp at Aldershot, England, and three Canadian soldiers were killed.[2] After this, the raids grew bigger and more frequent, striking several times a week at ships and ports on Britain's south coast. At this stage they did no major damage, except to coastal shipping.

By the end of July, Royal Air Force fighter planes had shot down around 180 German aircraft. They lost 70 of their own. Hitler was frustrated by the lack of success. He ordered his pilots "to overpower the English air force in the shortest possible time."[3] The *Luftwaffe* (German air force) began attacking airfields and aircraft factories.

THE BATTLE OF BRITAIN

The Germans called August 13 *Adlertag* (Eagle Day). They launched their biggest aerial campaign yet, aimed at defeating the Royal Air Force and making the invasion of the United Kingdom possible. This was the crucial period of what became known as the Battle of Britain, and one of the turning points of the war.

At the beginning of the conflict, the Royal Air Force had 507 single-engine fighters available, while the *Luftwaffe* had 703.[4] Though outnumbered, the British *Hurricane* and *Spitfire* aircraft were an even match for the German *Messerschmidt 109s*. However, the German fighters had two big disadvantages. They carried less fuel and had farther to fly than the British fighters. Also, they were fighting over foreign soil. If they survived a crash, they would be captured.

At least 1,485 German fighters and bombers crossed the English Channel on this first day, in several different attacks.[5] As the campaign continued, the Germans lost more aircraft than the British. They changed tactics again in late August and targeted only fighter bases in the United Kingdom. Somehow, the Royal Air Force survived.

THE BLITZ BEGINS

Even though the Germans were not winning the Battle of Britain, many bombers were getting through. London and other cities were badly damaged, and more than 1,000 civilians were killed during August.[6] Things were about to get much worse, though.

On September 7, there was a massive raid on the dockland area of London, which was a major center for cargo ships at the time. This was the beginning of the "Blitz," in which German bombs rained down on London for 76 consecutive nights. Many other British cities, including Liverpool, Glasgow, and Bristol, also suffered terrible damage. The Blitz did not end until May 1941.

▽ The German bombing raids destroyed large areas of British towns and cities, leaving many people homeless.

FIGHTING IN THE AIR

Planes had often been used in warfare before. During World War I, German *Zeppelin* airships had bombed parts of northern Europe, and fighter aircraft had fought against each other. However, planes had little impact on the course of that war. Since then, bombers had become much bigger and more effective, and fighters were faster and better armed.

THE FEW

Much smaller numbers took part in this aerial conflict compared with warfare on land. Fewer than 3,000 Royal Air Force pilots flew in the Battle of Britain (though they were supported by many other people, including ground controllers, radar operators, and mechanics). More than 400 of these pilots were killed in action.[7] As Churchill said afterward, "Never in the field of human conflict was so much owed by so many to so few." He meant that a very small number of pilots had saved a whole nation from invasion.

Who were the pilots?

Only about 80 percent of Royal Air Force fighter pilots in the Battle of Britain were actually British. Some came from countries already defeated by the Nazis—Poland, Czechoslovakia, and France. Others were from Australia, New Zealand, Canada, and other nations of the British Empire. There were also at least 10 pilots who came from the United States. They had volunteered, even though their country was still neutral.[8]

For more information on this, topic go to www.battleofbritain1940.net/0004.html.

△ During the Battle of Britain, Allied fighter pilots often flew on several missions every day.

WAITING TO SCRAMBLE

A Royal Air Force pilot on flying duty had a long, exhausting day. The threat of death or serious injury was constant. Even so, he might spend long periods at the base doing nothing except waiting to be sent into action at a moment's notice. Of course, not everyone returned from the missions. Some were killed when they were shot down, and others would have managed to parachute to safety.[9]

CRASH LANDING

On July 9, New Zealand pilot Al Deere took off from an airfield in Kent, England. He led his formation of *Spitfire* fighters out to attack German fighters. It was his fourth "**scramble**" of the day. In a dog fight, Deere's *Spitfire* collided with a German *Messerschmitt* aircraft. He remembered: "I could see puffs of smoke and the odd flame coming from the engine cowling, the engine began to vibrate.... Smoke started to pour into the cockpit."

The engine stalled, and through the smoke and flames Deere suddenly saw the ground rushing toward him. The *Spitfire* bounced, then plowed its way across a cornfield before stopping. Deere managed to escape, almost unhurt.[10] He had been amazingly lucky. Many pilots who were shot down suffered terrible injuries, including burns that crippled or disfigured them.

BREATHING SPACE

The start of the Blitz was yet another tactical change by the Germans. They were now starting to attack industrial towns instead of airfields. Their aim was to damage the manufacture of ammunition and other important supplies and to break civilian morale. This gave the Royal Air Force crucial breathing space. It had time to recover, train more pilots, and build new aircraft. In the end, this helped the United Kingdom to survive. Many historians believe the German change of tactics was a grave mistake and a turning point in the war.

The Royal Air Force was also helped by a new invention, not yet in use by the Germans. Radar used radio waves to detect the location and whereabouts of enemy aircraft.

The last great German attack of the Battle of Britain came on September 15. A huge force of bombers and fighters approached London. In desperation, the Royal Air Force sent all available fighters to meet them. Nearly 60 German aircraft were shot down, while the United Kingdom lost fewer than 30.[11] This was the end. Two days later, Hitler announced that he was postponing plans for Operation Sealion.

BOMBS IN THE DARK

The Germans had failed to destroy the Royal Air Force and gain control of the British skies. In fact, the Royal Air Force was now bombing major towns in Germany. Yet the Blitz on the United Kingdom continued—and got heavier. The bombers now came at night, which made them harder to spot. Dropping high explosives and firebombs, they devastated large parts of London and other cities.

People spent the night in shelters in their backyards or in communal bunkers. In London, hundreds took refuge in underground railroad stations. Many children were evacuated from towns to the country. By the end of 1940, another 500,000 evacuees had left London.[12]

VITAL SUPPLIES

The Battle of Britain was over, but the Battle of the Atlantic had barely begun. Goods from overseas were essential for a small island like the United Kingdom. Without raw materials and oil, its factories could not produce weapons. Without supplies of grain and other foods, its people would have starved within a few months.

⚠ Conditions on board a German U-boat were very cramped. The crew often had to stay at sea for long periods.

Churchill later admitted, "The only thing that really frightened me during the war was the U-boat peril."[13] U-boats were German submarines. This threat to cargo ships crossing the Atlantic was growing. The U-boats had begun hunting in packs of 10 or 12. Spread out across the surface, they could easily spot Allied convoys and then close in to attack them from underwater.

CALL-UP IN THE UNITED STATES

On the other side of the Atlantic Ocean, the United States was building up its armed forces, even though it was still officially neutral. In September 1940, the U.S. Senate passed a bill (law) making all men between the ages of 21 and 35 liable to be called up for military service. Soon, more than 16 million had registered. However, President Roosevelt remained publicly cautious. He told the people, "Your boys are not going to be sent into any foreign wars."[14]

CAMPAIGNS IN THE EAST

During its first year, the conflict was hardly a world war. The main fighting was confined to Europe and China, where the Japanese continued with their slow and bitter invasion into the south of the country. This changed at the end of 1940, and the war began to expand as many more countries became involved. Within another year, the fighting had spread to North Africa, the Mediterranean, the Balkans, Russia, and Indochina.

FALSE START FOR ITALY

Mussolini was anxious to get his soldiers involved in the action, but they were not well trained or equipped. In the fall of 1940, an Italian army invaded Egypt. It was soon driven out again by a much smaller but more mobile and well-trained force of British and Australian troops. The Italians also marched into Greece, only to be beaten back by a ferocious Greek counterattack.

Early in 1941, Hitler decided to take over the North African campaign. He sent over a collection of the troops and tanks he could spare in Europe to support the Italians. Led by Erwin Rommel, these German and Italian units began a long struggle against the British to gain control of Libya and Egypt. The force eventually became known as the Afrika Korps. (For all of this, see the map on page 16.)

BATTLE FOR THE BALKANS

Hitler had by now bullied several eastern European countries into joining the Axis powers. Some, such as Romania and Bulgaria, already had governments that supported the fascist cause. In Yugoslavia, however, many people rebelled against their government and demanded freedom. Hitler was furious and ordered an immediate invasion into the Balkans (the region in southeast Europe covered by the Balkan mountains).

During April 1941, German forces swept through Yugoslavia. At the same time, another Nazi army advanced into Greece from the east.

This encouraged the Italians, who made a second attack on Greece from the west. The British troops helping to defend Greece retreated to the island of Crete. By the end of May, the Germans had invaded Crete as well, with the main assault made by a huge force of paratroopers.

LEND-LEASE

Things were going badly for the Allies. The United Kingdom was alone in Europe and running out of money to buy weapons and raw materials. U.S. President Roosevelt declared that his country would be "the arsenal [supplier of weaponry] of democracy." He now gave much-needed help, pushing a new "Lend-Lease" law through Congress. This agreed to lend U.S.-made equipment to any country fighting the Axis powers. Gradually, the United States' involvement in the war was growing.

The Warsaw ghetto

The Nazis wanted to get rid of the Jews in the countries they invaded. An early plan was to pack Jewish people into enclosed areas, called **ghettoes**. The largest of these was established in the Polish capital, Warsaw, in October 1940. More than 400,000[1] Jews were crammed into the old Jewish district of the city, and a high wall was built to imprison them. Soon, thousands were dying of starvation, disease, and random killings by SS soldiers. There were dozens of other ghettoes in Nazi-ruled countries, including Hungary, Latvia, Czechoslovakia, and Russia.

◁ After the Germans created the ghetto for Jews in Warsaw in 1940, a wall was built to separate it from the rest of the city.

THE ENIGMA CODE-BREAKERS

By the 1930s, the Germans had developed a complex cipher (code) machine called Enigma. This turned messages into code so they could be transmitted by radio—without the enemy being able to understand them. If the Allies could break this code, they would have precious information about German plans and tactics.

HOW DID ENIGMA WORK?

A cipher is a system of coded writing, in which letters are rearranged or replaced to hide the meaning. An Enigma machine did this automatically. It had a keyboard, but inside was a series of discs, each containing a separate alphabet. When a letter key was pressed, the discs turned and changed to display a different letter.

▽ Women played an important part in the top-secret code-breaking work at Bletchley Park.

In this way, every letter in a message was changed, or **scrambled**. The Enigma operator could also alter the setting of the discs to make different combinations. In fact, the number of possible combinations was 159,000,000,000,000,000,000.[2]

THE POLISH BREAKTHROUGH

The Germans believed no one would solve their Enigma cipher. Soon, however, Polish agents made the first breakthrough. They had even built a special calculating machine, called a **bombe**. This stored all the possible letter combinations made by Enigma and automatically sorted through them until it found how the discs were set.

Before their country was invaded in 1939, the Poles passed this important information on to the secret services of the United Kingdom and France. It was an enormous help to the scientists already working to break the Enigma puzzle.

STATION X

The secret headquarters of the Allied code-breaking unit was at Bletchley Park in Buckinghamshire, England (officially known as Station X). Here, teams of scientists studied millions of coded German messages picked up by British radio receivers. By analyzing the messages, they were able to figure out ways of translating the cipher. The Germans did not know that the Enigma code had been broken.

By late 1941, analysts at Bletchley Park were **deciphering** 30,000 Enigma messages every month.[3] These included news about the location of U-boat packs, allowing Allied ships to avoid them.

Hundreds of people worked at Bletchley Park. Many, like this member of the women's branch of the British army, did dull but important jobs:

I worked in Hut 5, part of the Japanese Section. My job was to copy groups of letters onto large sheets of squared paper in different colored inks according to a code letter.... These sheets were collected by the code-breakers in the room next door. Other clerks in the hut were mainly male military personnel—men invalided from active service, others too old for active service, with clerical backgrounds—salesmen, bank clerks, etc.[4]

THE EASTERN FRONT

By mid-1941, Hitler had a firm grip on Europe. Only a weakened United Kingdom stood against him in the west. In the east, Germany controlled nearly all the land along the Soviet border. It was time for the next step in Hitler's master plan. He was going to invade his ally, the Soviet Union.

The Soviet Union had land and resources that would be needed by the growing German empire. The Nazis also saw Russia as the home of communists and Jews, both of whom they wanted to eliminate.[5] In fact, Hitler and Stalin had only signed their pact in 1939 in order to buy themselves more time to prepare for war.

The invasion, called Operation Barbarossa, was launched on June 22, 1941. It was the biggest of all *blitzkrieg* attacks. German tanks smashed their way through the Soviet defenses along the Eastern Front (see the map below), supported by aircraft and more than three million men. The Soviets were taken by surprise, and many thousands were captured in the first few days.

▷ In Operation Barbarossa, German forces attacked the Soviet Union along the massive Eastern Front.

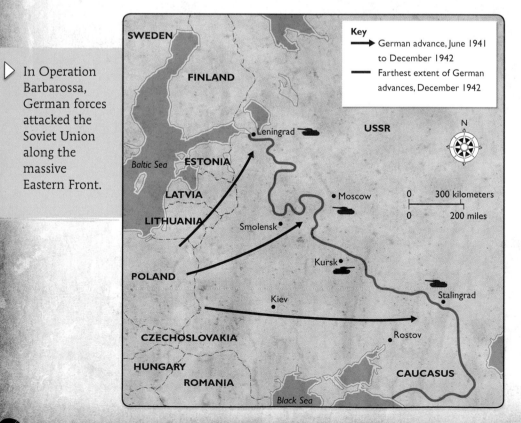

The Germans drove deep into Russia. By November 1941, they had advanced more than 700 miles (1,100 kilometers) from the border and were about to strike at two major cities, Leningrad (St. Petersburg) and Moscow. They had captured or killed more than two million Russians.[6] So far, the invasion was a triumph.

The Final Solution

The Nazi leaders had been planning the **extermination** of all European Jews since the start of the war. In July 1941, General Hermann Goering wrote about "the intended final solution of the Jewish question."[7] So what would this "final solution" be? During the invasion of Poland and Russia, the Germans rounded up countless thousands of Jews. Many were shot, starved to death in ghettoes, or worked to death as slaves. The Germans now planned a quicker and more systematic way of killing them. Jews and other minority groups would be rounded up and killed with poisonous gas. It was around this time that the first death camps with specially built gas chambers were constructed.

"MERCILESS, TOTAL ANNIHILATION"

The Nazis entered the Soviet Union determined to be more ruthless than ever before. A German general wrote that their aim was "the shattering of present-day Russia. Every combat action must be inspired by an iron determination to ensure the merciless, total **annihilation** of the enemy."[8]

From the start, Barbarossa was a shockingly savage campaign. The Germans killed not just enemy soldiers, but also whole civilian communities, and they burned down villages. Many resistance fighters were hanged, and prisoners and Jews were massacred. As the Germans advanced, Russian people destroyed factories, railroads, dams, and food supplies to stop them from falling into the hands of the Nazis. This "scorched earth" policy made it very difficult for the invaders to live off the land they conquered. Then, in December, snow started to fall and the advance was halted.

THE UNITED STATES ENTERS THE WAR

By late 1941, Germany's advance into Russia had come to a halt. On the other side of the world, Japan's campaign in China was also slowing down. However, the Japanese, frustrated in China, were already planning an even more ambitious war in which they could make massive gains very quickly. Their aim was to build a Japanese empire in Southeast Asia and the Pacific. To gain an important advantage, they were going to attack a new enemy: the neutral United States. This would make the conflict a truly global one.

AN EASY TARGET

On the morning of December 7, 1941, a Japanese fleet was just 275 miles (440 kilometers)[1] from Pearl Harbor, in the Hawaiian Islands. More than 180 war planes took off from the Japanese aircraft carriers, loaded with bombs and torpedoes. At Pearl Harbor they attacked the U.S. Pacific fleet stationed there as well as surrounding military installations. A second wave of aircraft followed swiftly, causing even more damage.

Within two hours, the attacks sank or damaged 19 warships, destroyed 188 aircraft, and killed more than 2,000 Americans.[2] The Japanese caught the U.S. Navy in the Pacific completely by surprise. Code-breakers in Washington, D.C., had intercepted Japanese messages that gave clues about their plans. Some historians have suggested that President Roosevelt knew about the attack before it happened and failed to take action. This has never been proven, and the claims are generally discounted.

WAR ACROSS ASIA

After the shock of Pearl Harbor, the United States could not stay neutral. The next day, President Roosevelt announced that his country, along with Canada and the United Kingdom, had declared war on Japan. Most Americans now supported him. Germany and Italy declared war on the United States soon afterward.

The attack at Pearl Harbor crippled the U.S. fleet—although its aircraft carriers remained intact, a factor that was to prove vital in fighting the Japanese at sea. This gave the Japanese freedom to expand their empire in Southeast Asia and the Pacific. They desperately needed access to land, raw materials, food, and fuel, and they wanted to drive the British and other European powers out of their Asian colonies.

Japanese troops moved quickly in several directions. They invaded Thailand, and they captured Hong Kong (governed by the British) and the Pacific islands of Guam and Wake (governed by the United States). By February 1942, they had driven through the Malayan jungles and stormed the British island of Singapore. The loss of Singapore, with the capture of 130,000 troops,[3] was the United Kingdom's worst defeat in World War II.

The Japanese advance seemed unstoppable. To the west, they gained control of Burma. To the south, they seized Java, Sumatra, and Borneo. Even Australia now felt itself under the threat of invasion. To the east, the Japanese drove U.S. forces out of the Philippines—though the U.S. commander, Douglas MacArthur, declared, "I shall return."

▽ Troops on both sides had to adapt to the difficult terrain of the jungle. The Japanese carried portable bridges, which were held up by soldiers while their fellow soldiers crossed.

PRISONERS OF THE JAPANESE

In western Europe, thousands of soldiers on both sides were taken prisoner. Most were treated humanely and survived the war. In Southeast Asia, however, things were very different. The Japanese had a strict military code that encouraged them to believe that a man should prefer to die rather than stop fighting against the enemy. So, Allied troops who surrendered were treated as people who had no right to live. This attitude was very different from that of most other countries during World War II, who usually respected the rights of prisoners.

BEATINGS AND BEHEADINGS

Japanese prisoner-of-war (POW) camps held soldiers and civilians from the United States, the United Kingdom, China, the Philippines, and other countries. Most camps were brutal places. Prisoners were starved, forced to work very hard, and savagely beaten for even small offenses against prison rules. Huge numbers were executed, and many more died from disease.

◁ This drawing shows prisoners of war building a bridge on the Burma-Thailand railroad.

A U.S. soldier who was held in a Japanese POW camp in northern China remembered what happened to prisoners who tried to escape: "They were brought back to our camp and dug their graves. Then the Japanese made all of us in the camp get out and stand there and watch them being shot and then they were buried right there."[4]

At least 27 percent of all prisoners in Japanese camps died.[5] Many of those who survived were little more than skeletons and never properly recovered. The camps were surrounded with barbed wire, with jungle beyond. Anyone who tried to escape might be beheaded.

In April 1942, U.S. and Filipino troops surrendered to the Japanese on the Bataan Peninsula in the Philippines. The 76,000 survivors[6] were then forced to march more than 60 miles (100 kilometers) to a camp in the north. The route took them over rough roads in extreme heat.

The nightmare journey lasted at least five days. During that time, prisoners had little food or water. Many were sick or wounded. The slowest were beaten, and any who dropped out of the line were murdered by "clean-up" squads following behind. At least 10,000 died during the death march, around 2,000 of them Americans.[7]

BUILDING THE BURMA RAILROAD

The Japanese planned a 260-mile (415-kilometer) railroad linking Burma and Thailand. To build it, they shipped thousands of Asian slaves, along with British, Australian, and Dutch prisoners to camps along the route in late 1942. The laborers had to work mainly by hand, building bridges, shifting rock, and laying track.

Exhaustion, **malnutrition**, disease, and Japanese violence took a huge toll. At least 12,600 Allied prisoners died during the construction of the Burma Railroad. Worse still, more than 85,000 Asians died (most of them Burmese or Malaysian)—half the total workforce.[8] There is no wonder it was called the Railroad of Death.

British soldier Jack Sharpe was one of the longest survivors in the prison camp near Changi, Singapore. He remembered:

I got scurvy [a disease caused by lack of vitamins], *which made my eyes like balls of fire, all matter coming out. My mouth was all swollen and red raw. I could barely swallow. I was covered in scabs from head to foot.*[9]

INTERNMENT CAMPS IN THE UNITED STATES

When Japan attacked Pearl Harbor in December 1941, there were many people of Japanese descent living in the United States. At least 110,000 lived on the West Coast.[10] Within a few weeks, all of these Japanese-Americans had been taken from their homes and placed in **internment** camps. Most stayed in the camps for three or four years.

Did you know?

At the start of the war, many thousands of people were interned in the United Kingdom. Most of these were Jews and other nationalities who had fled from mainland Europe. The vast majority were judged to be "friendly aliens" and were quickly released. Only around 8,000 were believed to pose a real threat, many of them of German and Italian descent. They remained in internment camps on the Isle of Man.

WHY WERE THEY LOCKED UP?

Immigrants from Japan had been arriving in Hawaii and the western U.S. states since the 1860s. Many settled permanently. Those who were born in Japan were called *Issei*, while second-generation Japanese Americans were *Nisei*. Most *Nisei* were full U.S. citizens.[11]

Even so, after Pearl Harbor they were all classified as "enemy aliens"—and possible enemies of the United States. White people believed they could be spying for the Japanese armed forces or plotting to help in an invasion of California. In February 1942, the U.S. federal government ordered that all Japanese residents in the states of California, Oregon, and Washington should be interned.

THE CAMPS

There were 10 internment camps in the western United States. All were in isolated locations, high in cold mountain regions, or in dry dusty deserts. The internees were taken there by train and then by bus

▽ Thousands of Japanese-Americans had to spend a long time behind the barbed wire fences of internment camps.

or even cattle truck. The camps were surrounded with barbed wire fences, and they had watch towers manned by armed guards.

One girl later described how she felt when reaching the camp: "We saw all these people behind the fence, looking out, hanging onto the wire.... I will never forget the shocking feeling that human beings were behind this fence like animals."[12]

The internees were not tortured, starved, or forced to perform hard labor, but it was still a terrible experience for them. They lived in cramped barracks and had to line up to get food, take showers, use toilets, and wash their laundry. The food and the sewage systems were often poor, and internees had little privacy. Worst of all, of course, was the loss of their freedom.

There were ways of getting out of camp, though. Internees could take on jobs or training courses that took them elsewhere. *Nisei* men of the right age were also able to volunteer for the armed forces. More than 17,000 joined,[13] many wanting to prove their loyalty to the United States.

HITTING BACK

In five months of fighting between 1941 and 1942, Japan had gained a massive stretch of territory. This included all of Malaya, Burma, and the Philippines, as well as large parts of Borneo and Indo-China (see the map on page 44). They had badly damaged the U.S. Pacific fleet and sunk several British warships. More than 250,000 U.S., British, and other Allied soldiers had been killed, wounded, or captured.[14]

In the middle of all this bad news for the Allies came a surprise counter-blow by the U.S. Air Force. In April 1942, a fleet of bombers took off from carriers in the Pacific. They flew over Japan and bombed the capital, Tokyo, and other cities. The raid did little damage, but it shocked the Japanese, who believed they were safe from air attack.

BIOGRAPHY

Franklin D. Roosevelt, 1882–1945

BORN: Hyde Park, New York

ROLE: President of the United States, 1933–45

As a young man, Franklin D. Roosevelt suffered from polio, which left him partly paralyzed. However, this did not stop him from becoming governor of New York and then president of the United States in 1932. His handling of the Great Depression made him popular, and he was reelected in 1936 and 1940. While the United States was neutral during the first part of World War II, Roosevelt spoke out against the Axis dictators and helped the United Kingdom and other Allies with arms and materials supplies. He was re-elected for a fourth term as president in 1944.

DID YOU KNOW? Roosevelt's cousin had also been president. Theodore Roosevelt was in the White House for two terms from 1901.

THE THREAT TO AUSTRALIA

The Japanese clearly intended to attack northern Australia. They had already bombed the town of Darwin, and in May 1942, a Japanese fleet set sail to attack Port Moresby, at the southern end of New Guinea. This would give them a perfect base for launching an invasion of Australia's Northern Territory.

U.S. warships hurried to intercept the Japanese attack in what was called the Battle of the Coral Sea. This was the first sea action in which all the fighting was done by aircraft, and the rival fleets never saw each other. There was no real winner, as each side lost only one major ship (aircraft carrier). However, the battle stopped the Japanese advance on Australia.

VICTORY AT MIDWAY

Next came one of the most important events of World War II. In early June, the Japanese sent an invasion force of more than 800 ships[15] to capture Midway Island, an important U.S. Navy base west of Hawaii. Once again, the U.S. fleet moved to stop them. Bombers were sent from carriers to attack the Japanese ships, but many of them were shot down.

Then a second wave of U.S. bombers took off. This time, they hit their target. Within a few minutes they had badly damaged four Japanese aircraft carriers, which later sank. The United States lost only one carrier. The Battle of Midway was a clear victory for the Allies, and it meant that Japan would not take control of the Pacific. The Americans could also build new carriers much more quickly than the Japanese, since they had much greater industrial resources.

◁ U.S. *Grumman Avenger* torpedo bombers were crucial strike aircraft when they were launched from carriers at sea.

THE TIDE TURNS

By late summer 1942, the war had reached its halfway point. So far, the Axis powers had been stunningly successful, but now things had begun to change, thanks to two major events. One was the entry into the war of the United States, with its mighty industrial power and growing armed forces. The other was the defiance of the Soviet Union, which first stopped and then drove back the invading Germans.

BOMBS ON GERMANY

The main Blitz on the United Kingdom had ended in 1941, but the Royal Air Force continued bombing German towns. At first, planes dropped bombs over a wide area, only hoping to hit important military targets, because their bombing techniques were not accurate enough. In May 1942, the Royal Air Force changed to launching much bigger attacks. Its first "thousand-bomber raid" dropped nearly 1,500 tons (1,360 tonnes) of bombs[1] and battered the industrial town of Cologne, Germany. Other enormous raids followed.

In August, U.S. bombers flew over Europe for the first time. A fleet of huge B-17 aircraft (nicknamed "Flying Fortresses") successfully attacked railroad yards in northern France. From this point on, Germany and its **occupied territories** suffered regular big bombing raids, which were designed to destroy the people's will to fight.

Flying into danger

Flying a bomber was one of the most dangerous activities in the war. Around 50 percent of U.S. and British bomber crews were lost as a result of going into action. This was a far higher death rate than that suffered by any other service in the war.[2] Altogether, more than 100,000 Allied bomber crewmen were killed over Europe.[3]

EL ALAMEIN

The Allies also achieved important success in North Africa. General Rommel and his Afrika Korps had aimed to seize the Suez Canal in Egypt. This would have cut off an important supply route for the Allies. But in July 1942, a major German and Italian advance into Egypt was halted by British troops near the town of El Alamein.

The leader of the Allied forces, General Bernard Montgomery, now prepared for the crucial battle of the campaign. He built up his troop strength, which included Australians, Indians, and South Africans, as well as British soldiers. He gained new equipment, such as Grant and Sherman tanks, much of which was supplied by the United States. On October 23, Montgomery went on the attack. After a long and exhausting battle, British and Australian troops broke through the enemy lines. Rommel retreated westward into Tunisia.

U.S. FORCES IN NORTH AFRICA

On November 8, another Allied force landed on the coasts of Morocco and Algeria. It consisted mainly of U.S. troops and was led by General Dwight Eisenhower. Advancing into Tunisia from the west, the Allies closed in on Rommel's German and Italian forces.

Once again, the struggle between the two sides was long and hard. Rommel began to run out of supplies, especially fuel for his tanks. The Germans were slowly pushed back toward the sea. They surrendered in May 1943, and 275,000 Axis soldiers became prisoners of war.[4]

▽ At El Alamein, Allied tanks advanced through gaps, cleared by their troops, in the German minefields.

THE FRENCH RESISTANCE

The fall of France brought hardship and fear to the French people. The Germans plundered their money, possessions, and food. Anyone who resisted was imprisoned or executed. Many were ashamed that their leaders had agreed to work with the Nazis. However, there were also plenty of French people who continued fighting against the occupiers.

THE *MAQUIS*

During the early years of the war, most resistance groups were based in towns and cities, but this made it easy for the Germans to trace them. From late 1942, many resisters moved to the forests and mountains of the deep countryside, where they could find hiding places. They became known as the *maquis*, a French word for "scrubland."

Fighters in the *maquis* operated in small groups. They lived in remote woods, barns, mountain huts, or abandoned churches. They got food from the local people, but they always had to be on watch in case they were betrayed to the Germans. British planes dropped supplies of weapons, ammunition, and explosives by parachute.

WHAT DID THEY DO?

The main aim of the Resistance was to make life difficult for the Germans and to help the Allies. They did this by:
- sabotaging sites that were useful to the occupiers, such as railroads, bridges, airfields, and ammunition stores
- rescuing Allied pilots who had been shot down in France and helping them escape to the United Kingdom
- ambushing and killing German soldiers and members of the *Milice* (the special French police force, similar to the *Gestapo*)
- intercepting German telephone and radio messages and passing them on to the United Kingdom
- helping French Jews to escape from France, to save them from being rounded up and sent to death camps.

Hiding in remote locations, the French *maquis* fought a guerrilla war against the German occupiers.

LONELINESS AND DEATH

Resistance fighters lived secretive and very dangerous lives, away from villages and other social centers. One man remembered how lonely he felt: "At dawn I saw chimney smoke coming up from Alés [a town]. I felt as if I were on another planet, isolated. I imagined life down there, people going to the [movies] . . . eating, listening to the radio. Surely they had forgotten us."[5]

They were also constantly at risk of death. Resistance fighters captured by the Nazis would probably be executed immediately. By the time France was **liberated** in 1944, 30,000 resisters had been shot, and another 20,000 had disappeared.[6] The Germans also killed many ordinary French citizens as punishment for the actions of the Resistance. In August 1944, for example, 124 out of 500 inhabitants of the village of Maille were shot by the Nazis in a revenge killing.[7]

BIOGRAPHY

Pearl Cornioley, 1914–2008

BORN: France

ROLE: British agent in France during World War II

Hundreds of Allied agents were smuggled into France to spy and to help organize the Resistance. Many, such as Pearl Cornioley, were women. She was born and raised in France to British parents and spoke fluent French. Parachuted into France in 1943, she ran a large network of Resistance fighters and helped sabotage a key railroad line 800 times.[8] She lived to be 93.

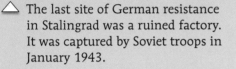

SURRENDER AT STALINGRAD

By the summer of 1942, the Germans had once again pushed the Russians back. Hitler believed that the Red Army had been beaten and was about to surrender. His armies were besieging the city of Leningrad (now St. Petersburg), and he now ordered General Friedrich von Paulus to attack Stalingrad (now Volgograd). The battle began in August and lasted for five months.

△ The last site of German resistance in Stalingrad was a ruined factory. It was captured by Soviet troops in January 1943.

German bombers caused huge damage to the city, and Paulus's troops tried to advance, but the Russians resisted. They made the Nazis fight for every street and house among the ruins. Then, suddenly a massive new Soviet army appeared and encircled the attackers. Starving and exhausted, the Germans were forced to surrender on January 31, 1943.

INVASION OF ITALY

Soon afterward came the surrender of the Germans in North Africa, another big defeat for Hitler. This meant the Allies were now free to cross the Mediterranean and attack southern Europe. In July 1943, a huge Allied force under General Eisenhower landed on the south coast of Sicily. After weeks of bitter fighting, the island was captured. By this time, Mussolini had fallen from power and had been imprisoned by the new Italian government.

By early September Italy had surrendered and was out of the war. Eisenhower's armies invaded the Italian mainland and began moving north. However, the Germans quickly brought in their own troops. They released Mussolini, occupied the city of Rome, and blocked the progress of the Allies.

ALLIED AIR POWER

The Germans were also losing the Battle of the Atlantic. They were sinking fewer Allied ships and losing many more U-boats. One reason for this was new technology such as sonar echolocation, which helped pinpoint submarine positions underwater. Another was the growing use of special U.S. attack planes to search out and destroy Nazi submarines.

U.S. and British bombers were also destroying important Axis targets. In August U.S. aircraft flying from North Africa raided oilfields in Romania. This damaged an important supply of fuel for German tanks and factories.

Holocaust resistance

All over Europe, the Germans were herding Jews, **Roma**, and other minority groups into death camps. Against impossible odds, some prisoners now fought back. In January 1943, Jews in the Warsaw ghetto launched an armed uprising against the Nazis. In August, inmates at the Treblinka camp killed their guards, and many escaped. In October, women at Auschwitz attacked soldiers as they were being taken to the gas chambers. The Nazis crushed these revolts with great brutality, but the actions sent out a powerful message of defiance.

BIOGRAPHY

Joseph Stalin, 1879–1953

BORN: Georgia, Russia

ROLE: Leader of the Soviet Union

Born the son of a shoemaker, Stalin became a leading communist. Imprisoned in Siberia for organizing strikes, he was released after the Russian Revolution in 1917. During the 1920s, Stalin became Soviet leader. He ruthlessly killed or jailed all who opposed him. Several million people died during his long period in power. However, his cunning and strong leadership enabled the Soviet Union to be one of the most important factors of the Allied victory in World War II.

THE ALLIES ADVANCE

By 1943 World War II was slowly swinging toward the Allied side. In Russia, the Germans were being driven back by the Red Army. The Italians had surrendered. The Japanese had been forced to stop their expansion in the Pacific and East Asia. The Allies had begun their invasion of southern Europe. However, the struggle was taking a terrible toll on soldiers and civilians on both sides.

NEW GUINEA

The Japanese had been trying to conquer New Guinea for many months. This would give them an important base from which to attack Australia. Australian and other Allied soldiers prevented their advance, though, and then pushed them to retreat. Soon the Japanese had been forced into a small area in the south of New Guinea, short of ammunition and food. They were finally defeated in January 1943.

Next, the Allies attacked enemy positions on the northern coast. The Japanese sent a large convoy of warships, troops, and supplies to help fight off the attack. This was wiped out by low-flying U.S. and Australian bombers. By the end of 1943, Allied forces controlled almost all of New Guinea.

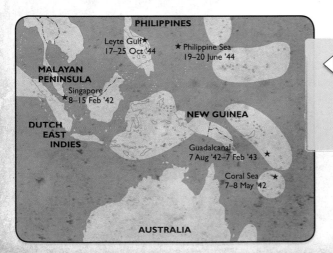

PHILIPPINES

Leyte Gulf★
17–25 Oct '44

★ Philippine Sea
19–20 June '44

MALAYAN
PENINSULA

Singapore
★8–15 Feb '42

DUTCH
EAST
INDIES

NEW GUINEA

Guadalcanal
7 Aug '42–7 Feb '43 ★

Coral Sea ★
7–8 May '42

AUSTRALIA

Here you can see some of the main sites of the war in the Pacific region.

ISLAND HOPPING

In July 1943, U.S. and other Allied troops started a series of carefully planned assaults on island groups in the Central Pacific. One force landed in the Solomons, taking one island after another. A second force targeted the Gilbert Islands to the north. The aim was to work their way toward the Mariana and Philippine Islands, the groups closest to Japan itself.

The campaign used a technique called island hopping. The Allies seized an island and secured a base, then "hopped" on to the next. They did not attack every island, though. Instead, they learned to "leapfrog," bypassing islands with strong Japanese defenses and invading those that were easier to capture quickly.

BATTLING THROUGH BURMA

Meanwhile, on the Asian mainland, other Allied forces were struggling to drive the Japanese out of Burma. The interior of the country, with its mountains, jungles, and swamps, was very hard to move and fight in. In 1943, the Indian Army advanced along the coast, but it was soon forced to retreat. Chinese forces, led by U.S. General "Vinegar Joe" Stilwell, advanced slowly from the northeast. Stilwell's main aim was to open up a route across Burma and into China for desperately needed supplies.

In 1944, the Japanese sprang a new surprise. They crossed the western border into India and surrounded Allied forces in Imphal and Kohima. The defending army included British, Indian, and African soldiers as well as Gurkhas (soldiers from Nepal). After weeks of bitter fighting, the Japanese were forced to retreat. The Allies pursued them back into Burma in late 1944.

Fighting in the jungle

Rain forest (jungle) was probably the most difficult kind of terrain for warfare. Soldiers had to move through dense undergrowth, where few vehicles could go. Mules were often used to carry equipment. The climate was mostly hot and very wet, causing disease to spread and clothing and equipment to rot. Then there was the danger from poisonous insects and snakes, not to mention bigger predators.

THE HOME FRONT: LIVING AND STRUGGLING THROUGH WAR

World War II brought death, fear, hardship, and hunger to places far away from the front line. For the first time, a large number of civilians discovered that being a long distance from the battle did not mean they were safe. The "home front" became a very important part of the conflict. How did British, German, and U.S. people experience this terrible period, from their opposing sides?

WAR HITS HOME

The United Kingdom was not invaded during World War II, but it was attacked. Enemy aircraft flew overhead and dropped bombs on towns and cities. A million people left London and other city areas to find refuge from the bombs. Londoners lost nearly a third of their houses.[1] Near the end of the war, the Germans launched unmanned "flying bombs" and rockets across the English Channel. U-boats sank Allied cargo ships carrying important supplies of food and raw materials.

Germany was not invaded until 1944, but German cities also suffered heavy bombing raids throughout most of the war. This caused the same kind of tragedies as in the United Kingdom. However, the Blitz on Germany was far heavier and went on for longer. More than 400,000[2] German civilians died as a result of bombs during the war. The total in the United Kingdom was around 70,000.

As the war went badly for Germany in 1943, far more evacuees had to move. More than 1 million people left Berlin during September alone.[3] Victims lost their homes and had to find somewhere else to live. Over time, Berlin was hit very badly. By late 1944, a quarter of all the city's houses had been destroyed.[4]

⚠ Huge areas of Hamburg in Germany were
destroyed by repeated Allied bombing raids in
1944 and 1945.

THE HOME FRONT IN THE UNITED STATES

Although the United States did not suffer from direct attacks to its
home front, the lives of ordinary citizens were still deeply affected by
the war. Here are some of the main changes:

- *Tax increases*: Taxes rose to pay for the growing war effort—some by as
  much as 10 percent between 1940 and 1944.
- *Rationing*: There were shortages of many everyday items, which were
  rationed by the government. Among the rationed items were car
  tires, shoes, sugar, meat, and coffee.
- *The draft*: Huge numbers of men were drafted into the armed
  forces. The size of the U.S. forces rose from 1.6 million in 1941 to
  11.4 million in 1945.
- *Women at work*: Women joined the national workforce, many for
  the first time. In many branches of industry, such as factories,
  they replaced men who were on combat duty. This gave women a
  significantly stronger role in the U.S. economy than ever before.
- *Civilian patrols*: Civilian spotters were recruited to work part-time,
  looking out for enemy aircraft and working on search-and-rescue
  missions. Others patrolled towns, making sure that windows were
  blacked out at night in case of enemy raids.

THE TRIUMPH OF THE RED ARMY

With their great victory at Stalingrad, the Russians had stopped the Nazi advance to the east. Now the Red Army slowly began to push the Germans backward. In July 1943, it secured another major victory at Kursk, in Russia, where it destroyed a huge force of German tanks. By January 1944, the Red Army had broken the siege of Leningrad. Hitler's forces were now in retreat.

How had the Red Army achieved this astonishing turnaround? A key reason was the massive Russian population. Despite the huge numbers of soldiers killed or captured by the Germans, the Soviets were always able to fill their places with new recruits (including women soldiers). Soviet factories were also producing tanks and other heavy weapons at great speed, aided by materials from the United States and United Kingdom. In addition, Russia had substantial supplies of many natural resources, including iron and coal.

BLOCKING THE WAY NORTH

Meanwhile, in southern Europe, the Allied march into Italy had come to a halt. The Germans had built a line of defensive positions across the narrow Italian peninsula to block the path to Rome. From January 1944, U.S. and British troops battled to cross this line at Monte Cassino, a monastery high in the mountains. Despite heavy bombing and shelling, they could not break through.

◁ In 1944 it took the Allied invasion force four months to capture the monastery at Monte Cassino, in southern Italy.

The Allies also tried to outflank the enemy by making a landing farther up the west coast, at Anzio, Italy. However, the Germans kept the landing party pinned down and unable to move for four months. Monte Cassino finally fell to the Allies in May. The Allied forces had been strengthened by fresh troops, and it was Polish and North African soldiers who stormed the mountain and took the monastery. The long fight for Monte Cassino had cost the Allies dearly, however: 31,000 men had been killed, wounded, or captured.[5]

THE BIG THREE

An Allied victory now seemed possible for the first time during the conflict. The three main Allied leaders—Churchill, Roosevelt, and Stalin—flew to a summit meeting in Teheran, Iran, at the end of November 1943. The aim of the "Big Three" was to agree on a strategy for what they hoped was the final stage of World War II.

Churchill explained the plans for a British- and U.S.-led invasion of northern France the following spring or summer. The task would be easier, he said, if the Red Army continued to launch strong attacks in the east. This would prevent the Germans from moving reinforcements from there into France. Stalin agreed and promised that the Soviet Union would join the other Allies in the war against Japan "the moment Germany is defeated."[6]

Beware of the Greeks

Every occupied country had resistance fighters, but few matched the dramatic deeds of the Greeks in early 1944. First, in February, freedom fighters used explosives to blow a troop train into a flooded river in northern Greece. More than 400 Nazi soldiers died.[7] Then, in April, guerrillas led by British agents kidnapped the German commander in Crete and smuggled him out to Egypt.[8]

49

THE INVASION OF EUROPE

On June 6, 1944, Allied forces landed in Normandy, on the coast of northern France. It was the biggest seaborne invasion in history, and it opened up an enormous new battle front in the west. At the same time, on the Eastern Front, the Red Army was about to smash its way into Poland and the Baltic countries. In the south, the Allies had marched into Rome, Italy's capital. Everywhere, it seemed the Germans were in retreat.

OPERATION OVERLORD

The Normandy landings, named Operation Overlord, had taken four years of top-secret planning. The amount of organization involved was staggering. More than 850,000 Allied soldiers, with their weapons and equipment, landed on a 50-mile (80-kilometer) stretch of coast. This was achieved by 8,000 aircraft, 1,200 warships, and the work of three million men.[1]

△ Dummy tanks and other equipment were assembled in parts of southern England to confuse the Germans about the exact location of the D-Day landings.

Most of the Allied troops met powerful resistance from the Germans. Beaches were blocked with barbed wire, metal stakes, landmines, and other obstacles. German guns kept up heavy and deadly fire. In some places, the invaders were trapped for hours on the shoreline. Progress was very slow. It took six weeks for the Allies to capture the major Normandy towns of Cherbourg and Caen.

The invading force did not break away from the coast until late July. Then, after bombers had blasted a hole in the German lines, the Allies poured through into central France. One army, under Montgomery, cleared the Nazis from the northwest. Another, under General George S. Patton, headed for the French capital, Paris.

Many Parisians started an uprising against the Nazis, which was savagely crushed. More than 3,000 French fighters died, as well as 2,000 Germans.[2] At last, on August 25, the Allies marched in to liberate Paris from the Germans, who had retreated without trying to defend the city. At their head was a division of French troops.

THE SOUTHERN AND EASTERN FRONTS

Meanwhile, in Italy, Allied forces captured Rome in June and Florence in August. At the same time, U.S. and French troops landed on the south coast of France, near Cannes. Southern France fell very quickly, as Hitler sent his soldiers to help defend the north.

In the east, the Soviets had launched a series of assaults on the German defenses. The attacks were made by an astonishing 1.2 million men, supported by thousands of tanks, artillery, and aircraft. Within six weeks, they had advanced 300 miles (480 kilometers), to the outskirts of Warsaw in Poland. It was a disaster for Hitler, as more than 350,000 of his troops were killed, wounded, or captured.[3]

Hitler survives a bomb plot

On July 20, 1944, Hitler was at his headquarters in Rastenburg, Germany. A bomb had been placed under his conference table. It exploded, wounding Hitler but not killing him. The plotters, a group of senior German army officers, were arrested, and most of them were shot immediately. They had wanted to kill Hitler because they realized he was leading Germany to a catastrophic defeat.[4]

LIVING THROUGH D-DAY

D-Day began at 6:31 a.m. on the morning of June 6, 1944. It was a day late. D-Day had been planned for June 5, but it had been delayed by bad weather. In Britain, the invading soldiers had already been waiting for hours, many crowded onto warships or waiting at airfields. Most of them were scared and tired. So, what was it like to go into such an immense and crucial battle?

LANDING IN FRANCE

Simply getting safely onto French soil was highly dangerous, whether you came by sea or by air. The main types of transportation were:

- *Landing craft:* These boats were shallow, so they were tossed around by the waves. Many men were soon seasick, and often they landed in deep water. A U.S. soldier wrote: "It was up to my shoulders when I went in, and I saw men sinking all about me. There were bodies floating everywhere ... facedown in the water with packs still on their backs."[5]

- *Glider:* Troops were packed into gliders, which were towed into the sky by powered aircraft and released. Pilots steered the gliders to land at specially selected spots. This was very hard, as a British pilot recalled: "My objective was a small corner of a tiny field. If I overshot, I would crush us all against a high embankment. If I undershot, I would destroy my seven tons of powerless aircraft and its human cargo on a belt of trees. There was no room for error."[6]

- *Parachute:* Paratroopers were dropped behind enemy lines to seize bridges and other key sites near the landing areas. Sometimes, like this U.S. paratrooper, they descended in the wrong place: "When my parachute opened, I was directly above the church steeple of the church in Sainte Marie du Mont. The moon was full and there were scattered clouds which made everything on the ground easy to see." He managed to land safely and helped in the capture of the village, a very important event of D-Day.

△ General Dwight D. Eisenhower (left) was supreme commander of the Allied forces during the invasion of France. His deputy was Field Marshal Bernard Montgomery (right).

DEATH ON THE BEACHES

Once on the ground, Allied attackers were the target of ferocious German gunfire. They were faced with a hail of shells from machine guns, **mortars**, field guns, and rifles from strong defensive positions. They also had to get through wire entanglements and minefields. There was little cover on most of the beaches, and large numbers of men were trapped in the sand and shingle (small stones).

It was just as terrifying for the defenders. This German soldier (speaking in English) described his experience: "There was thousands of ships, and we could see landing boats. Then came thousands of men on land running over the beach. This is the first time I shoot on living men, and I go to the machine gun and I shoot, I shoot, I shoot! For each American I see fall, there came ten hundred other ones!"[7]

D-Day casualties

The following are figures for the dead, wounded, and missing:

	Allies	Germans	French civilians
D-Day (June 6)	10,000	4,000–9,000	[not known]
Battle of Normandy (June 6–30)	209,000	200,000 (plus 200,000 captured)	15,000–20,000[8]

To find out more about D-Day, go to www.dday.org.

DISCOVERING THE DEATH CAMPS

The most terrible atrocity of World War II was the Nazi program to wipe out the European Jews. Included in this slaughter were other groups of people, such as the Roma and homosexuals. Altogether, nearly six million Jews and others perished in what the Nazis called "the Final Solution," and what we now know as "the Holocaust."

SECRET SLAUGHTER

During the war years, the Germans gradually developed a system of mass extermination, which they wanted to be quick and cheap. Victims were taken in large groups from their home areas to specially built camps, often by railroad. There, most of them were killed with poison gas and their bodies were burned in ovens. The rest were beaten, starved, or worked to death.

The Italian writer Primo Levi survived the hell of Auschwitz (a network of camps in Poland) and saw the inner strength of many of his fellow prisoners. He wrote: "We are slaves, deprived of every right, exposed to every insult, condemned to certain death, but we still possess one power, and we must defend it with all our strength for it is the last—the power to refuse our consent."[9]

Ordinary people in Allied countries knew almost nothing about the Nazi death camps. Not surprisingly, the Germans were anxious to keep their existence a secret. However, Allied governments were well informed from an early stage. Their code-breakers intercepted radio messages about the camps, and agents in German-held territory sent back reports. What the Allies did not know was the horrific scale of the slaughter.

THE POLISH DEATH FACTORIES

On August 25, 1944, an Allied reconnaissance aircraft took aerial photographs of an oil processing plant in southern Poland. It also photographed an unidentified camp outside the nearby town of Auschwitz. At the time nobody realized the significance of these pictures. With later knowledge, of course, it was seen that they clearly showed gas chambers, **crematoria**, a train, and a line of prisoners.

Auschwitz was in fact the Nazis' main death camp, and it had been in operation gassing prisoners since 1942. Jews from all over occupied Europe arrived here by train, and as many as 24,000 were killed every day.[10] There were five other extermination camps in Poland, including Sobibor and Treblinka. Inside Germany were others used for mass killings, such as Buchenwald and Belsen.

▷ Advancing Allied troops were shocked by the scenes they found in the Nazi death camps, such as Buchenwald in Germany.

As the Germans began to retreat on the Eastern Front in 1944, they tried to destroy evidence of the "Final Solution." The camps were emptied, and the gas chambers and other buildings were blown up. All those prisoners who could walk were herded together and marched into Germany. The rest were shot or left to die.

Soviet troops reached Auschwitz on January 27, 1945. They found more than 600 dead bodies and 7,000 starving survivors.[11] As Allied forces advanced through Poland and Germany during the following weeks, they discovered more crowds of exhausted and half-dead Jews in other extermination camps, as well as many thousands of corpses.

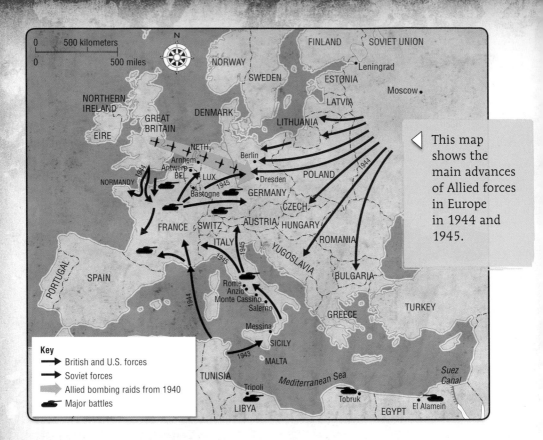

This map shows the main advances of Allied forces in Europe in 1944 and 1945.

TOKYO COMES WITHIN BOMBING RANGE

The war in East Asia had now reached a crucial stage. U.S. and other Allied forces had driven the Japanese from most of the Central Pacific. In June 1944, they began their attack on the Mariana Islands. The U.S. Pacific fleet shattered the Japanese navy in the Battle of the Philippine Sea off Guam, sinking three carriers and destroying 480 aircraft (see the map on page 44).[12]

This sea victory opened the way for U.S. land forces to capture the Marianas. The Allies now had an island base only 1,500 miles (2,400 kilometers) from Japan itself. This was within flying reach of US B-29 long-range bombers. By the fall, these bombers were making regular raids on Tokyo and other Japanese cities.

The next step was the liberation of the Philippine Islands. In October a huge Allied invasion force landed on the island of Leyte. Among the 100,000 U.S. soldiers to walk ashore was General Douglas MacArthur, who had kept his promise from 1942 ("I shall return").

The Japanese navy made its final attempt to defeat the U.S. fleet. The Battle of Leyte Gulf was the biggest naval battle in history, with 282 ships from both sides.[13] It was also decisive. After three days, the Americans had destroyed the Japanese fleet, sinking many ships, including their last four aircraft carriers. This ended the threat from Japan's navy. Many of their trained pilots had also been killed.

The Germans were also facing defeat. In eastern Europe, the Red Army continued to advance, pushing into Romania and Bulgaria. By November it began the invasion of Hungary, Germany's last big ally in Europe. Meanwhile, the Nazis were withdrawing troops from Yugoslavia and Greece, in the face of ferocious resistance fighting. The Greek capital, Athens, was liberated in October.

THE BATTLE OF THE BULGE

However, Hitler had one last surprise for the Allies. He had planned an assault in western Europe, through the Ardennes forest into Belgium. Even his commanders thought it was hopeless, especially as dead soldiers were now being replaced by untrained young teenagers and older people. "All Hitler wants me to do," said one, "is to cross a river, capture Brussels, then go on and take Antwerp. All this when the snow is waist deep and with divisions made up chiefly of kids and sick old men—and at Christmas."[14]

However, the offensive took the Allies by surprise on December 16, 1944. The U.S. units in the Ardennes were swept aside, but the Germans lacked enough troops and fuel to get far. The Allies halted their advance at the Meuse River in Belgium. In this operation, called the Battle of the Bulge (because it created a bulge in the Allied front line), Hitler lost 45,000 troops[15] and most of his armored forces.

Flying bombs

In June 1944, the Germans launched a new kind of weapon against the United Kingdom. Called the V-1, it was a flying bomb powered by a jet engine that cut out after a certain distance, making the bomb crash to earth. Thousands of V-1s bombarded southeast England, killing more than 6,000 people. In November, London and other northern European cities were also hit by the first V-2s, which were high-speed rockets.

SURRENDER

By the beginning of 1945, the Axis powers were in a hopeless position. In Asia, U.S. bombers were pounding Japanese cities and industrial regions. Allied troops were strengthening their hold on the Philippines, while others were driving the Japanese out of Burma. In Europe, Germany had lost nearly all its conquered territories, and the Allies were closing in from all sides. The end was in sight.

Yalta

The "Big Three" Allied leaders held another summit meeting in February 1945. This took place at Yalta, on the Black Sea coast of Russia. With victory in sight, they made decisions about what the post-war world would look like. For example, Germany would be divided into four zones, each occupied by a different Allied power (France was the fourth).

INTO GERMANY

On January 31, 1945, the first of the Allied forces crossed the German border. This was the Soviet Red Army, which pushed its way to the banks of the Oder River, only 40 miles (64 kilometers) east of the capital city, Berlin. The British and Canadians came from the north, having chased the Germans from the Netherlands. By early March, they had joined U.S. and French troops from the west on the Rhine River.

The Rhine was the last big obstacle for the Allies. Hitler had ordered most bridges to be destroyed, to stop them from crossing. Some were still intact, though, and on March 7, U.S. soldiers reached the bridge at Remagen just as the Germans were about to blow it up. They charged over and became the first Allies across the Rhine. They were soon followed by many more.

IWO JIMA

Some of the fiercest fighting of the war was now taking place on the tiny Pacific island of Iwo Jima, just 750 miles (1,210 kilometers) from the Japanese coast. The Americans had landed on February 19, after a three-day bombardment of the island by battleships. Their progress was slow across the rocky and barren island.

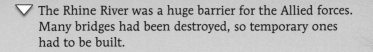

The Japanese troops defended from a network of caves and tunnels, all of these soldiers determined to die rather than surrender. They would hide underground during the U.S. bombardment, then emerge unharmed to fire from cover. U.S. troops found that ordinary gunfire was not effective in this landscape, so they increasingly used flame throwers instead, because the flames could reach inside the caves.

Iwo Jima was not taken until March 16, when U.S. soldiers captured its two airfields. At least 20,000 Japanese defenders had died, leaving only a few who were too badly wounded or weak to commit suicide. More than 6,800 U.S. soldiers had been lost, as well as 900 sailors who drowned when a carrier was sunk.[1]

FIRESTORMS

Allied bombing of Axis territories became heavier. The German and Japanese air forces were now too weak to be a serious threat to U.S. and British bombers. In Europe and Japan, almost daily raids did huge damage to enemy towns, transportation systems, and industrial areas.

One of the most horrific attacks was the attack on the German city of Dresden on February 14. High explosive and **incendiary bombs** caused a **firestorm** that killed more than 50,000 people.[2] On March, 10 U.S. *B-29 "Superfortress"* bombers brought even greater slaughter to Tokyo, Japan. At least 83,000 people died, and large areas of the city were flattened.[3]

THE SOVIETS REACH BERLIN

The Allied armies were now racing across Germany from west and east, as Nazi resistance collapsed. In March 1945, U.S. commander Dwight Eisenhower realized that Soviet forces would reach Berlin first. He halted his armies on the Elbe River, about 60 miles (100 kilometers) west of the German capital.

This allowed the Red Army to attack Berlin alone in mid-April. Its tanks surrounded the city. After two days of shelling and aerial bombing, Soviet troops began to fight their way toward the center. By April 29, the battle was almost over. Nazi soldiers saw that their situation was hopeless, and so they started to surrender in large numbers.

On the afternoon of April 30, Adolf Hitler was in his bunker in central Berlin. The Soviets were only a mile away, and their shells were raining down. Hitler handed over command of Germany to three of his deputies, then he committed suicide by taking a poison capsule and shooting himself. His body was burned.

April had also seen the deaths of two other war leaders. U.S. President Roosevelt had died on April 12. His position was taken by the vice-president, Harry S. Truman. On April 28, the deposed Italian dictator Benito Mussolini was shot dead by resistance fighters. His body was hanged upside-down in the center of Milan, Italy.

VICTORY IN EUROPE

On the day of Hitler's suicide, Soviet troops captured Germany's government building, the Reichstag. Most of the German forces had now surrendered. The Red Army surged through Berlin, looting, killing, and assaulting the citizens. The soldiers were hungry for revenge—not just for the 500,000 fellow soldiers killed since they crossed the German border,[4] but also for the Nazi invasion of Russia in 1941.

On May 4, the new German leaders began peace talks with the Allies. Three days later, they signed the documents of surrender, and on May 8, the war in Europe officially ended. "Victory in Europe" (VE) Day was celebrated wildly in the streets of London, New York, Paris, Moscow, and other Allied capitals.

JAPAN FIGHTS ON

However, the war had not stopped in Asia. While Europe rejoiced, Allied and Japanese armies were still fighting fiercely. British, Indian, and other troops from the British Empire captured Rangoon, the capital of Burma, in early May. Australian soldiers continued their long battle to take control of Borneo and New Guinea.

Meanwhile, U.S. forces were edging nearer to Japan itself. In April, landing parties invaded the island of Okinawa, just 340 miles (540 kilometers) from the Japanese mainland. It was a slow and bitter struggle against a defending army of about 120,000, but in late June, Okinawa fell. More than 110,000 Japanese were killed or committed suicide, many by jumping from cliffs into the sea. The United States lost 12,500 men.[5]

Kamikaze attacks

In a last, desperate bid to win the war, the Japanese air force recruited a team of suicide pilots in late 1944. Their orders were to fly planes packed with explosives directly into U.S. naval vessels. Named *kamikaze* (the Japanese for "divine wind") missions, these suicide bombings caused heavy damage, putting several warships out of action.

DROPPING THE ATOMIC BOMB

In the early morning of August 6, 1945, a U.S. B-29 bomber took off from Tinian Island, in the Marianas in the Pacific. Five and a half hours later, its crew released an atomic bomb over the Japanese city of Hiroshima. It was the first time a nuclear weapon had been used in wartime, and it opened up massive and horrifying new possibilities for warfare in the post-war world.

BUILDING THE BOMB

In 1939 leading scientists warned President Roosevelt that Germany might be developing a terrible new weapon. This used the enormous power within an atom, which might be released by splitting the nucleus (central part) of an atom. It was possible that an "atomic" bomb could be made using radioactive material such as uranium.

The U.S. government knew it had to develop its own atomic weapon before the Germans, or face defeat. So in 1942 it set up a secret operation run by U.S. and European scientists to research and build a nuclear-splitting bomb. Called the Manhattan Project, this was based in sites all over the United States. A test device was successfully exploded in the New Mexico desert in July 1945.

HORROR IN HIROSHIMA

The first atomic bomb, slowed by a parachute, **detonated** over Hiroshima at 8:16 a.m. Japanese time. Within seconds there was a flash of intense brightness and heat, followed by a gigantic shockwave. Here are some of the terrible things people felt and saw in the city:

Ah, that instant! I felt as though I had been struck on the back with something like a big hammer, and thrown into boiling oil.—Schoolgirl

Near the bridge there were some who were burned black and died, and others with huge burns who died with their skin bursting.—Six-year-old boy

△ Over 78,000 people died in Hiroshima immediately after the atomic bomb detonated. A total of 140,000 had died by the end of 1945 as a result of the attack.

As I came to the river, I found that the stream was filled with dead bodies. I started to cross by crawling over the corpses. —Businessman

There was a charred body of a woman standing frozen in a running posture with one leg lifted and her baby tightly clutched in her arms. —19-year-old girl[6]

WHY DID THE ALLIES USE ATOMIC BOMBS?

The Allies wanted to finish the war as soon as possible, but the Japanese government refused to surrender. The death tolls on Iwo Jima and Okinawa had been appalling, and it seemed certain that a land invasion of Japan would take a long time, killing huge numbers more on both sides. On top of this, thousands of people were dying in the frequent bombing raids on Japanese towns.

Allied leaders believed that dropping the atomic bomb would save time and lives. However, even after the terrifying destruction at Hiroshima, the Japanese delayed their surrender. On August 9, the United States dropped a second nuclear weapon, this time on the city of Nagasaki. The effects of these two attacks are still being felt today, as victims continue to die of sickness caused by **radiation** from the blasts.

JAPAN SURRENDERS

Even after the bombing of Nagasaki, the Japanese government could not agree about surrender. Some government officials were determined to continue fighting, even though the cause was hopeless. Unable to reach a decision, the leaders consulted with the country's emperor, Hirohito. This was an extraordinary move, because the emperor was regarded as a god and rarely involved himself in government matters. Hirohito told them the time had come "to bear the unbearable"[7] and lay down their arms.

On August 15, several Japanese government officials and commanders committed suicide to avoid the shame of surrender. The same day, Hirohito spoke to his people by radio for the very first time. He said the war "had turned out not necessarily to Japan's advantage," and that the enemy were now using "a new and most cruel bomb."[8] Without mentioning the word "surrender," he declared that the Japanese must accept peace.

On September 2, Japanese leaders (but not the emperor) came on board the U.S. warship the USS *Missouri*. In front of Allied officers, they signed the documents of Japan's official surrender. World War II was over, after almost exactly six years of fighting and bloodshed.

GETTING HOME

Hundreds of thousands of prisoners of war in Europe and Asia were now free, but getting back home would prove to be a long and difficult journey. Many POWs never recovered from their horrific treatment at the hands of the Japanese and died before they could be sent home. Others did not reach their native lands until the following year.

Victory over Japan Day

As soon as Japan's surrender was announced, people in Allied countries around the world began joyful celebrations that peace had come at last. Huge crowds paraded through the streets, danced to the honking of taxis, lit bonfires, and set off fireworks. Thousands of soldiers, sailors, and airmen joined in the rejoicing. National leaders, including Britain's King George VI and U.S. President Truman, broadcast speeches to their people.

△ Soldiers, sailors, airmen, and civilians celebrated VJ Day in every Allied country.

A far greater number of civilians had fled their homes or been forcibly moved during the war. In Europe alone, there were 20 million[9] of these "displaced persons." Many were Jews and other minority groups who had survived the Nazi death camps and ghettoes. All wanted to return to their own countries or find safe places to live. Large numbers eventually got home, but many remained permanently displaced.

PUNISHING THE WAR CRIMINALS

As peace returned, more and more evidence was found showing that terrible war crimes had been committed. These included several "crimes against humanity," such as genocide, deporting people for slave labor, and other inhuman acts. Between 1947 and 1953, more than 500 Germans[10] and 920 Japanese[11] were tried and executed for their offenses.

Twenty-two of the surviving Nazi leaders were tried at a special court in Nuremberg, Germany, between 1945 and 1946. Among them were Hermann Goering, head of the *Luftwaffe*, and Rudolf Hess, who had been Hitler's deputy. Most were found guilty, and 11 were sentenced to death. Goering poisoned himself before his execution. Hess was sentenced to life imprisonment and lived on until 1987.

WHAT HAVE WE LEARNED?

World War II ended in 1945, but the world was not at peace. Many local fights continued—some of them created by the war, some merely interrupted by it. There were soon civil wars in Greece, Korea, and China, as well as savage struggles for independence in India and Indonesia. The establishment of a Jewish homeland (Israel) in Palestine caused violence between settlers and Arabs. In many parts of eastern Europe and the Middle East, the drawing of new borders after the war brought about growing problems.

WHO WON AND WHO LOST IN THE POST-WAR YEARS?

- The Axis powers were of course the main losers of the war. Germany and Japan had shattered economies, with towns, industries, and commercial systems destroyed. Yet within 20 years they had both recovered, rebuilding cities and factories and becoming major manufacturing and financial powers.
- The United Kingdom and France ended the war as victors, but they were worse off than before. Both were exhausted by the war effort and were desperately short of materials, manpower, and money. They had also lost much authority throughout the world because they had been unable to protect people in their empires, especially the inhabitants of Malaya and Singapore. These empires, the source of much wealth, were about to disintegrate.
- The United States was a big winner. Starting the war with a small army, it rapidly developed a massive and well-equipped set of armed forces that could project its power around the world. It also changed from an isolated, neutral country into a superpower with nuclear weapons. This made the United States the leader of the "free" (non-communist) world. Thanks to a long economic boom, the United States also became one of the wealthiest and most industrially strong countries in the world.
- The Soviet Union was one of the biggest winners of the war. The Red Army's mighty advance from the east gave the Soviets total

control over eastern Europe, allowing them to establish communist governments there. This created a giant "bloc" of communist states, tightly ruled from Moscow. The war had also driven the Soviet Union to make massive developments in technology and industry. It swiftly grew into the world's second superpower.

- China was on the winning side, but was still an economically undeveloped country. The long Japanese invasion had caused enormous damage, and this was followed by an extensive civil war. The communist side won this struggle and established the People's Republic of China in 1949.

THE COLD WAR

So Europe, like Germany itself, was divided in two. In 1946 Winston Churchill spoke of an "Iron Curtain" descending across the continent. On one side were the free, capitalist nations of the West. On the other was the communist bloc. The communists stopped free travel between east and west. The United States pledged itself to oppose the spread of **communism** to other countries of the world.

The tensions between East and West quickly increased. Both sides began building up stocks of nuclear weapons. This was the start of what was called the Cold War (because it did not result in direct battles between the two sides). This conflict, with the constant threat of nuclear war, loomed over the post-war world. It lasted for several decades and only ended when the Soviet Union broke up in 1991.

UNITING FOR A SAFER WORLD

Despite these failures, world governments since World War II have searched for ways to prevent another global war. New bodies have been set up to increase cooperation and understanding between nations. The most notable of these is the United Nations (UN), created in October 1945. Almost every sovereign state in the world is a member. The main aims of the UN are to promote and maintain peace in conflicted areas, to uphold human rights, and to help the social and economic development of poorer countries.

TIMELINE

January 30, 1933	Hitler is appointed chancellor of Germany.
August 1934	Hitler becomes *führer* (dictator) of Germany.
March 1935	Hitler begins to build up German armed forces.
September 1935	The Nuremberg Laws in Germany take away many rights of Jews.
March 1936	German troops occupy the Rhineland.
May 1936	Italy invades Abyssinia (modern Ethiopia).
March 13, 1938	Germany forms a union (*Anschluss*) with Austria.
October 1938	Nazi troops occupy the Sudetenland region of Czechoslovakia.
November 9, 1938	"*Kristallnacht*" is a widespread night of violence against German and Austrian Jews.
March 15, 1939	Germany invades Czechoslovakia.
August 23, 1939	Germany and the Soviet Union sign a non-aggression pact.
September 1, 1939	German begins its "*blitzkrieg*" invasion of Poland.
September 3, 1939	The United Kingdom and France declare war on Germany. World War II begins.
April 9, 1940	Germany launches an invasion of Denmark and Norway.
May 1940	Germany invades the Low Countries and then France. Winston Churchill becomes British prime minister.
June 10, 1940	Italy joins the war on Germany's side.
June 14, 1940	The Germans take Paris.
June 22, 1940	France signs an armistice with Germany.
July–October 1940	The Battle of Britain begins. German bombing raids on British towns begin.
October 1940	Nazis establish a Jewish ghetto in Warsaw.
March 11, 1941	U.S. President Roosevelt signs the Lend-Lease Bill, making the United States a partner of the United Kingdom.
April 1941	German troops begin invasions of Yugoslavia and Greece.
June 22, 1941	Hitler launches Operation Barbarossa against the Soviet Union.
December 7, 1941	Japanese aircraft attack the U.S. Pacific fleet in Pearl Harbor, Hawaii.

December 8, 1941	The United States and United Kingdom declare war on Japan.
December 15, 1941	Japan begins invasions of the Philippines, Burma, and other Pacific countries.
February 15, 1942	The United Kingdom surrenders Singapore to the Japanese.
March 9, 1942	The Japanese capture Java.
April 18, 1942	The first U.S. bombing raid on Tokyo occurs.
June 6, 1942	The U.S. Navy defeats the Japanese at Midway.
November 6, 1942	The Allies achieve victory at El Alamein, North Africa.
January 31, 1943	German forces surrender at Stalingrad.
May 13, 1943	German forces in North Africa surrender.
July 1943	The Soviets achieve victory over the Germans at Kursk. U.S. forces begin to recapture the Solomon Islands and Gilbert Islands. The Allies land in Sicily.
September 8, 1943	Italy surrenders to the Allies.
January 1944	The Soviets relieve the German siege of Leningrad.
March 1944	The Japanese cross the Indian border and besiege Imphal.
June 5, 1944	The Allies liberate Rome, Italy.
June 6, 1944	D-Day: The Allies launch a massive invasion in Normandy, France.
June 20, 1944	The U.S. Navy defeats Japan in the Battle of the Philippine Sea.
August 25, 1944	Paris is liberated.
October 20, 1944	U.S. forces land on the Philippines.
December 16, 1944	Germans counterattack in northern France in the Battle of the Bulge.
March 1945	U.S. forces capture Iwo Jima. Allies cross the Rhine into Germany.
April 22, 1945	Soviet troops enter Berlin, Germany.
April 30, 1945	Hitler commits suicide.
May 8, 1945	Germany surrenders. It is VE (Victory in Europe) Day.
June 1945	U.S. forces capture Okinawa.
Aug. 6 and 9, 1945	U.S. aircraft drop atomic bombs on the Japanese cities of Hiroshima and Nagasaki.
August 15, 1945	Japan surrenders. It is VJ (Victory over Japan) Day.
September 2, 1945	Japanese leaders sign the surrender documents. World War II officially ends.

GLOSSARY

annihilation destruction or complete wiping-out of something

armistice truce, or stopping of fighting (but not a full surrender)

bombe electrical and mechanical device used by Allied code-breakers to help decode messages sent by German Enigma machines

bunker fortified place, often underground

communism social and political system in which property and the means of production are owned by the people of the country

crematorium (plural: crematoria) building containing furnaces for burning dead bodies

decipher convert a message from its coded form

depression (economic) time of drastic decline in an economy, with falling trade, prices, and employment

detonate set off a bomb or other explosive device

dictator ruler who has complete control over a nation and its people

evacuate leave or depart from a place

extermination get rid of something by destroying it completely

fascism system of government in which control is in the hands of extreme right-wing and nationalist rulers

firestorm violent storm caused by hot air rising from an area that is on fire. The resulting high winds make the flames burn more fiercely.

genocide planned destruction of a racial or political group of people

ghetto section of a city where Jews or other minority groups were confined during World War II

holocaust	widespread or horrific destruction of human life. ("The Holocaust" now refers specifically to the mass killings of Jews and others by the Nazis.)
incendiary bomb	bomb that scatters flammable material, which ignites and causes widespread fires
internment	forced confinement of a group of people within a country
liberate	free or release an area from oppressive enemy rule
malnutrition	illness caused by lack of a well-balanced diet
mortar	small cannon used to fire shells in a high arc over short distances
Nazi	member of the *Nationalsozialistische* (National Socialist) political party brought to power by Hitler
neutral	not joining either side in a conflict or dispute
occupied territory	area of land conquered and ruled by a foreign power
Parliament	law-making body in the United Kingdom
radiation	emission of particles from radioactive materials
rationing	system of distribution that allows someone to buy a fixed amount of food or other goods during a time of national shortage
refugee	person forced to flee his or her home due to war, natural disaster, or other violent events
Roma	traveling people who speak the Romany language; they are also known as "gypsies"
scramble	(aircraft pilots) to take off as quickly as possible to engage the enemy
scramble	(message encoding) to distort or garble a signal or message so other people will not be able to read it
Soviet Union (USSR)	federation (group) of communist states that dominated eastern Europe and North Asia from 1922 until its breakup in 1991
swastika	cross with the ends of the arms bent at right angles, used as an emblem by the Nazi Party in Germany
totalitarian	type of government in which total control of the population is imposed by repressive rulers

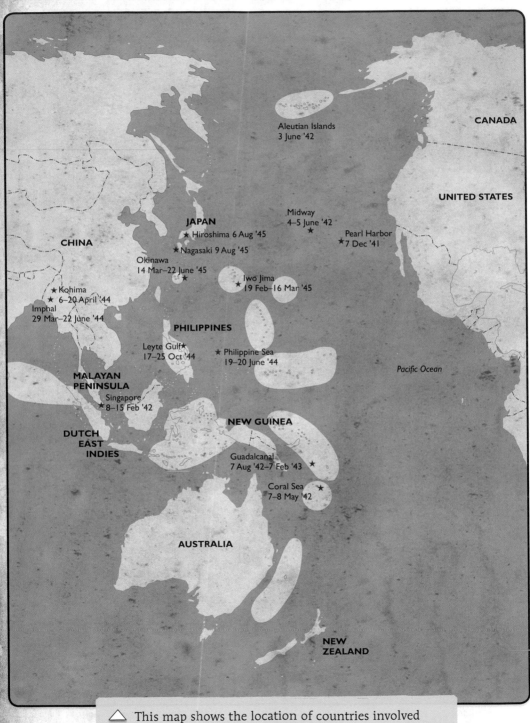

CANADA

UNITED STATES

Aleutian Islands
3 June '42

Midway
4–5 June '42
★

Pearl Harbor
★ 7 Dec '41

JAPAN
★ Hiroshima 6 Aug '45
★ Nagasaki 9 Aug '45

CHINA

Okinawa
14 Mar–22 June '45
★

Iwo Jima
★ 19 Feb–16 Mar '45

★ Kohima
★ 6–20 April '44
Imphal
29 Mar–22 June '44

PHILIPPINES

Leyte Gulf ★
17–25 Oct '44

★ Philippine Sea
19–20 June '44

Pacific Ocean

MALAYAN
PENINSULA

Singapore
★ 8–15 Feb '42

DUTCH
EAST
INDIES

NEW GUINEA

Guadalcanal
7 Aug '42–7 Feb '43 ★

Coral Sea ★
7–8 May '42

AUSTRALIA

NEW
ZEALAND

△ This map shows the location of countries involved
in World War II, and the sites of some major battles.

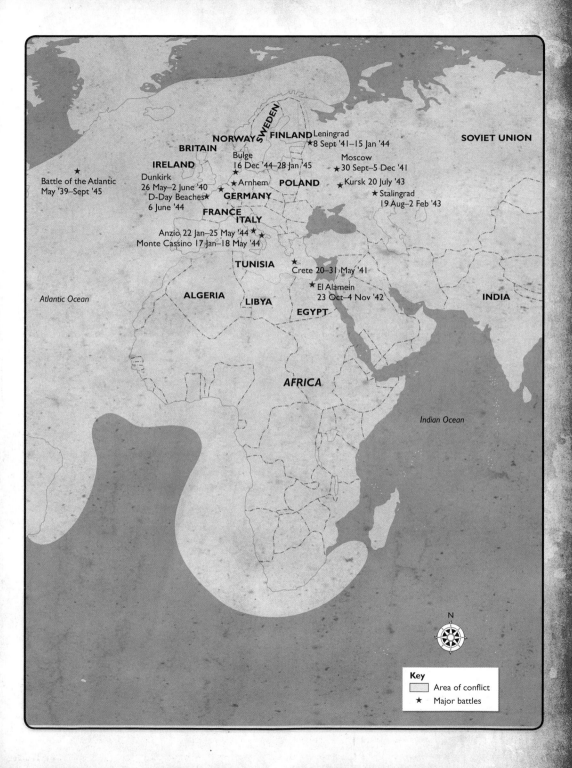

NORWAY
SWEDEN
FINLAND
Leningrad
★8 Sept '41–15 Jan '44

BRITAIN
IRELAND

Battle of the Atlantic
May '39–Sept '45 ★

Bulge
16 Dec '44–28 Jan '45

Moscow
★ 30 Sept–5 Dec '41

SOVIET UNION

POLAND
★ Kursk 20 July '43

Dunkirk
26 May–2 June '40
D-Day Beaches★
6 June '44

★ Arnhem
GERMANY

★ Stalingrad
19 Aug–2 Feb '43

FRANCE
ITALY
Anzio 22 Jan–25 May '44 ★
Monte Cassino 17 Jan–18 May '44

TUNISIA

Crete 20–31 May '41

★ El Alamein
23 Oct–4 Nov '42

ALGERIA
LIBYA
EGYPT

INDIA

Atlantic Ocean

AFRICA

Indian Ocean

N

Key
Area of conflict
★ Major battles

73

NOTES ON SOURCES

The Path to War (pages 4–9)
1. John Keegan, *The Second World War* (London: Hutchinson, 1989), 590.
2. http://www.time.com/time/world/article/0,8599,2023140,00.html.
3. Gordon Corrigan, *The Second World War: A Military History* (London: Atlantic Books, 2010), 81.
4. Piers Brendon, *The Dark Valley: A Panorama of the 1930s* (London: Jonathan Cape, 2000), 392.
5. http://www.dw-world.de/dw/article/0,,4201589,00.html.
6. Ian Kershaw, *Hitler 1889-1936: Hubris* (New York: W. W. Norton, 1999), 152.
7. Piers Brendon, *The Dark Valley*, 464.
8. Leonard Baker, *Days of Sorrow and Pain* (New York: Oxford University Press, 1978), 231.

A Lightning War (pages 10–17)
1. John Keegan, *The Second World War*, 81.
2. Alistair Horne, *To Lose a Battle: France 1940* (London: Macmillan, 1969), 397.

Struggle to Survive (pages 18–23)
1. John Keegan, *The Second World War*, 94.
2. Martin Gilbert, *Second World War* (London: Weidenfeld & Nicolson, 1989), 108.
3. John Keegan, *The Second World War*, 95.
4. Gordon Corrigan, *The Second World War*, 112.
5. Martin Gilbert, *Second World War*, 117.
6. *Ibid*, 122.
7. Len Deighton, *Fighter: The True Story of the Battle of Britain* (London: Jonathan Cape, 1977), 280.
8. *Ibid*.
9. http://www.battleofbritain1940.net document-17.html.
10. *Ibid*.
11. *Ibid*, 266.
12. Derrik Mercer (ed.), *Chronicle of the Second World War* (Longman, 1990), 130.
13. John Keegan, *The Second World War*, 104.
14. Martin Gilbert, *Second World War*, 135.

Campaigns in the East (pages 24–29)
1. Martin Gilbert, *Second World War*, 130.
2. Simon Singh, *The Code Book: The Secret History of Codes and Code-Breaking* (London: Fourth Estate, 2000), 157.
3. http://www.cl.cam.ac.uk/research/security/Historical/hinsley.html.
4. www.mkheritage.co.uk/bpt/women/wrensOS.html.
5. Gordon Corrigan, *The Second World War*, 137.
6. *Ibid*, 167.
7. William L. Shirer, *The Rise and Fall of the Third Reich: A History of Nazi Germany* (London: Secker & Warburg, 1959), 964.
8. Gordon Corrigan, *The Second World War*, 153.

The United States Enters the War (pages 30–37)
1. John Keegan, *The Second World War*, 255.
2. Derrik Mercer, *Chronicle of the Second World War*, 248.
3. John Keegan, *The Second World War*, 261.
4. http://www.chinadaily.com.cn/china/2007-05/26/content_881003.htm.
5. Yuki Tanaka, *Hidden Horrors: Japanese War Crimes in World War II* (Boulder: Westview Press, 1996), 2.
6. http://www.eyewitnesstohistory.com/bataandeathmarch.htm.
7. John Campbell (ed.), *The Experience of World War II* (London: Harrap, 1989), 125.
8. http://www.mansell.com/pow resources/camplists/death_rr/movements_1.html.
9. Max Arthur, *Forgotten Voices of the Second World War* (London: Ebury Press, 2007), 147.
10. http://www.smithsonianeducation.org/educators/lesson_plans/japanese_internment/index.

11. Gordon Corrigan, *The Second World War*, 512.
12. http://www.americanhistory.si.edu/ perfectunion/transcript.html#camps1.
13. Gordon Corrigan, *The Second World War*, 513.
14. *Ibid*, 282.
15. *Ibid*, 339.

The Tide Turns (pages 38–43)
1. John Campbell (ed.), *The Experience of World War II*, 178.
2. http://www.nationalarchives.gov.uk/ education/worldwar2/theatres-of- war/western-europe/investigation/ hamburg/sources/photos/2a/.
3. http://www.angelfire.com/ct/ ww2europe/stats.html.
4. John Keegan, *The Second World War*, 343.
5. H. R. Kedward, *In Search of the Maquis: Rural Resistance in Southern France 1942-1944* (Oxford: Oxford University Press, 1993), 234.
6. Ian Ousby, *Occupation: The Ordeal of France 1940-1944* (John Murray, 1997), 217.
7. http://acroy.perso.neuf.fr/home.htm.
8. http://www.guardian.co.uk/ world/2008/mar/06/colombia.

The Allies Advance (pages 44–49)
1. http://www.archnews.co.uk/ featured/4108-evidence-of-bomb- damage-from-ww2-part-2.html.
2. http://www.history.co.uk/explore- history/ww2/bombing-offensive.html.
3. Derrik Mercer, *Chronicle of the Second World War*, 440.
4. John Campbell (ed.), *The Experience of World War II*, 179.
5. Gordon Corrigan, *The Second World War*, 416.
6. Derrik Mercer, *Chronicle of the Second World War*, 467.
7. *Ibid*, 493.
8. *Ibid*, 510.

The Invasion of Europe (pages 50–57)
1. Donald Corrigan, *The Second World War*, 416.
2. Derrik Mercer, *Chronicle of the Second World War*, 555.
3. John Keegan, *The Second World War*, 391.

4. *Ibid*, 395.
5. http://www.eyewitnesstohistory.com/ dday2.htm.
6. Max Arthur, *Forgotten Voices of the Second World War*, 114.
7. http://www.pbs.org/wgbh/amex/dday/ sfeature/sf_voices_07.html.
8. http://www.ddaymuseum.co.uk/faq. htm.
9. Primo Levi, "If This Is a Man" (1947), quoted on http://www.goodreads.com/ author/quotes/4187.Primo_Levi).
10. John Campbell (ed.), *The Experience of World War II*, 216.
11. Martin Gilbert, *Second World War*, 634.
12. Derrik Mercer, *Chronicle of the Second World War*, 536.
13. *Ibid*, 576.
14. John Keegan, *The Second World War*, 441.
15. Gordon Corrigan, *The Second World War*, 538.

BIBLIOGRAPHY

Arthur, Max. *Forgotten Voices of the Second World War*. London: Ebury Press, 2007.

Campbell, John (ed.). *The Experience of World War II*. London: Harrap, 1989.

Corrigan, Gordon. *The Second World War: A Military History*. London: Atlantic Books, 2010.

Deighton, Len. *Fighter: The True Story of the Battle of Britain*. London: Jonathan Cape, 1977.

Gilbert, Martin. *Second World War*. London: Weidenfeld & Nicolson, 1989.

Keegan, John. *The Second World War*. London: Hutchinson, 1989.

Kershaw, Ian. *Hitler 1889–1936: Hubris*. New York: W. W. Norton, 1999.

Kershaw, Ian. *Hitler 1936–1945: Nemesis*. New York: W. W. Norton, 2001.

Mercer, Derrik (ed.). *Chronicle of the Second World War*. Burnt Mill, England: Longman, 1990.

Ousby, Ian. *Occupation: The Ordeal of France, 1940–1944*. London: John Murray, 1997.

Rhodes, Richard. *The Making of the Atomic Bomb*. New York: Simon & Schuster, 1986.

Shirer, William L. *The Rise and Fall of the Third Reich: A History of Nazi Germany*. New York: Simon & Schuster, 1959.

FIND OUT MORE

BOOKS

Adams, Simon. *DK Eyewitness: World War II*. New York: Dorling Kindersley, 2007.

Ambrose, Stephen E. *The Good Fight: How World War II Was Won*. New York: Athenaeum, 2001.

Calvocoressi, Peter, Guy Wint, and John Pritchard. *The Penguin History of the Second World War*. New York: Penguin, 1999.

Connolly, Sean. *Witness to History: World War II*. Chicago: Heinemann Library, 2003.

Dowswell, Paul. *Introduction to the Second World War: Internet Linked*. Tulsa, Okla.: EDC, 2005.

Murray, Doug, and Anthony Williams. *Graphic Battles of World War II: D-Day: The Liberation of Europe Begins*. New York: Rosen Central, 2008.

Zullo, Allan, and Mara Bovsun. *Survivors: True Stories of Children in the Holocaust*. New York: Scholastic, 2005.

DVDS

Documentaries

The War (2007)
This seven-part PBS series by Ken Burns focuses on how the war affected the lives of families in the United States.

The World at War (1973)
This classic history of the war comes in 26 parts.

Movies

Band of Brothers (2001)
This television series is about a U.S. infantry unit at the time of D-Day.

Saving Private Ryan (1998)
This movie tells the story of World War II from the perspective of U.S soldiers caught in the middle of the action.

Das Boot (1981)
This German movie provides an intimate picture of life in a German U-boat.

The Bridge on the River Kwai (1957)
This drama is set in a Japanese POW camp during the building of the Burma Railroad.

A Bridge Too Far (1977)
A Bridge Too Far is a realistic account of the disastrous landing at Arnhem in 1945.

Schindler's List (1993)
The harrowing tale of survivors from the death camps is portrayed in this movie.

The Thin Red Line (1998)
This movie is a fictional story of experiences during the battle for Guadalcanal.

WEBSITES

www.pbs.org/thewar/
This PBS website is a companion to Ken Burns's documentary series about the war. It is full of facts, photos, interviews, and more.

www.pbs.org/perilousfight/
This PBS website contains rare, fascinating color images from the war.

www.holocaust-history.org
This site tells the horrific tale of the war against Europe's Jews.

www.pcf.city.hiroshima.jp/index_e2.html
This site contains moving information and pictures about the legacy of the atomic bomb.

www.archives.gov/research/military/ww2/photos/
This National Archives site is full of interesting photographs from the war.

www.worldwariihistory.info/in
This website has wide-ranging facts about the conflict, particularly relating to U.S. involvement.

INDEX